The Healthy

Instant Pot Pressure Cooker Cookbook

120 Nourishing Recipes For Clean Eating, Paleo, AIP, Gluten Free, Vegan And Other Healthy Diets

PAULA COREY

ISBN-13: 978-1519768704

ISBN-10: 1519768702

DEDICATION

To JoAnn, for being an exemplary leader and shining a light on the path for us to follow.

TABLE OF CONTENT

Read Other Books By Paula Corey:

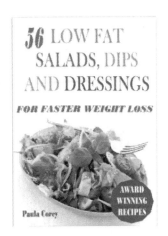

56 Low Fat Salads, Dips And Dressings For Faster Weight Loss

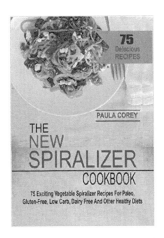

The New Spiralizer Cookbook: 75 Exciting Vegetable Spiralizer Recipes For Paleo, Gluten-Free, Low Carb, Dairy Free And Other Healthy Diets

The New Dutch Oven Cookbook: 105 Fresh Ideas For The Most Versatile Pot In Your Kitchen

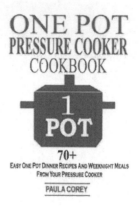

One Pot Pressure Cooker Cookbook: 70+ Easy One Pot Dinner Recipes And Weeknight Meals From Your Pressure Cooker

INTRODUCTION

The Instant Pot is known popularly as a pressure cooker. However, this versatile kitchen appliance provides many tools in one. It can be used for a variety of cooking tasks, including slow cooking, rice cooking, food warming, steaming, sautéing, browning and yogurt making. Buying and Instant Pot will also help to save a lot of room in your kitchen.

The focus of this book is the primary function of the Instant Pot, which is pressure cooking. Furthermore, this book only contains healthy recipes. While the recipes in this book can be enjoyed by all, they have been carefully selected to cover a range of dietary needs – **Clean eating, Paleo, AIP, Gluten free, Vegan and other healthy diets** so you can easily find the recipe that is right for you.

May meals can be cooked at the push of a button with the many micro-processor controlled intelligent programs. The microprocessor monitors the pressure and temperature during cooking and makes necessary adjustments. Each program can also be adjusted according to specific cooking requirements. This is the appliance for you if you lead a fast-paced life but still want your meals to be healthy.

The new technology of the Instant Pot makes it easy-to-use, safe and dependable. The 24 hour timer is great for planning meals ahead of time. Sautéing or browning can be done with 3 different temperature settings. The warming function helps to keep your food warm until you are ready to eat.

The cooking programs of the Instant Pot have been tested to ensure that you always produce delicious food every time. If you are new to pressure cooking, it may take a while to perfect your recipes. However, the Instant Pot takes away all the worries of beginners since the cooking programs will do most of the work for you. You will never have to worry about producing a wonderful meal.

Instant Pot Safety

Safety used to be a pressing concern with old types of pressure cookers. This is no longer a concern with the new types of pressure cookers because technological improvements have made it possible to address these safety concerns.

The following are the 10 safety mechanisms built into the Instant Pot:

Safety Lid Lock – To prevent accidental opening when the cooker is pressurized.

Lid Close Detection – Uses a magnetic sensor to check whether the lid is closed properly.

Pressure Regulator – To ensure that the pressure is maintained below the safety limit of 15.23psi.

Smart Detection – To detect leaky lead (for example, steam release is at the open position).

Automatic Pressure Controller – To keep pressure in the safe range.

Excess Pressure Protection – Excess pressure is released into the internal chamber when there is a dangerous situation.

Automatic Temperature Control – Regulates temperature according to the type of food.

High Temperature Monitoring – To avoid the burning of food.

Anti-Blockage Vent Design – To minimize blocking of vent by food residue.

Electrical Current And Temperature Fuse – To cut off power if the internal temperature or current exceeds safety limits.

Tips For Using Your Instant Pot Pressure Cooker

The following are some tips that will help you to make the best use of your Instant Pot pressure cooker:

You Can Cook Most Meals Using The "Manual" button

If you are confused by the program modes (Soup, Poultry, Meat/Stew, etc), your best option is to use the "Manual" button.

Simply press the "Manual" button and adjust the cooking time, using the plus and minus buttons. The cooker will start cooking automatically in 10 seconds. The default pressure cooking temperature is high. If the recipe specifies Low Pressure, use the "Pressure" key to toggle between "High Pressure" and "Low Pressure" as necessary.

Changing The Cooking Pressure

Most recipes specify High pressure while a few require Low pressure. Certain tender foods require low pressure cooking to avoid overcooking. High Pressure is the default for all functions of the Instant Pot except "Rice". Use the "pressure" button to adjust the cooking pressure. Start by pushing the "Manual" button (or applicable program), then push the "pressure" button until it displays "Low". You can then adjust cooking time with the "+" and "-" keys.

Safe Lid Opening: Three Ways

Before attempting to open the lid, ensure that the pressure cooking program is completed. You can also terminate the program by pressing "Keep-Warm/Cancel".

Quick Release - This releases pressure instantly. Press [Cancel] then twist the steam release handle on top of the lid to "Venting". Steam will be released and the float valve will drop down.

Caution for Quick Release:

- The steam is very hot, so keep your face and hands away from the hole on top of the steam release handle.

- While steam is being released, do not pull out the steam release handle.

- Do not use Quick Release for foods with large liquid volume (soup, porridge, etc) to avoid splattering of steam. Instead, use Natural Release.

10-minute Natural Release - Allow the pressure cooker to go into the Keep-Warm/Cancel mode then count 10 minutes. After 10 minutes, press [Cancel] and twist the steam release handle on top of the lid to "Venting". The remaining steam will be released and the float valve will drop down.

Natural Release - At the end of the cooking time, press [Cancel] and wait for about 20 minutes. The pressure will come down on its own and the lid will un-lock. If the cooker is very full, it may be more than 20 minutes. You can speed up cooling by putting a wet towel on the lid.

Pay Attention To Timing

For best results, follow the cooking times and the opening methods specified for each recipe.

Sauté Mode Heat Settings

When using the Sauté mode, you can control the heat level with the "Adjust" button. The three levels are:

"Normal": ~160°C (320°F) for regular browning,

"More": ~170°C (338°F) for darker browning, and

"Less": ~105°C (221°F) for light browning.

You can use "Normal" for most things, "Less" for simmering and "More" for boiling.

Minimum Amount of Liquid for the Instant Pot

1 cup is the minimum amount of liquid. However, absorbent foods like rice will require more water. Just follow what is indicated in the recipe.

Keep The Pot Half Full For Beans and Grains

The Instant Pot should not be filled more than half way when you are cooking beans or grains. They require adequate room to expand.

Release Pressure Carefully When You Cook Beans And Grains

Beans and grains generate a lot of foam, therefore it is better to use natural release when you cook them. This is to avoid foam spraying out of the valve. If you choose to use Quick Release, do it slowly. Stop to allow the foam to come out of the pressure release valve then continue after about 30 seconds.

Save Cooking Liquid For Other Recipes

Cooking liquid from vegetables contain a lot of vitamins and minerals. This nutritious liquid can be saved (refrigerated) and used as stock for other recipes.

Converting Recipes For Stove Top Pressure Cookers

If you have recipe books for traditional stove top pressure cookers (15 psi), simply add about 20% to the cooking time when using the Instant Pot. This is because the Instant Pot operates at 11.6 psi (High Pressure). For instance, 20 minutes becomes 24 minutes.

Getting More Knowledge

Read the manual that comes with your model of Instant Pot and contact support whenever you have questions.

Once you start using an Instant Pot pressure cooker, you will wonder how you survived without one before. It is a great time saver and makes healthy, flavorful meals because the nutrients are locked within the food and not lost.

BREAKFAST AND BRUNCH

Hard Boiled Eggs (Clean eating, Paleo, Gluten Free)
The Instant Pot gives you an easier way to hard boil eggs.

Preparation time: 3 minutes

Cooking time: 8 minutes

Servings:

Ingredients:

Pasture raised eggs

1 cup water

Directions:

1. Add 1 cup of water to the Instant Pot then put in the steamer basket.

2. Place the number of eggs that you want to cook into the steamer basket.

3. Cover with lid and set the valve to "seal". Choose "Manual" and adjust to 8 minutes cooking time at high pressure.

4. At the end of the cooking time, use the quick release method to release the pressure. Transfer the eggs to the refrigerator and use with your meals.

Breakfast Quinoa (Gluten free)

Preparation time: 3 minutes

Cooking time: 1 minute

Servings: 6

Ingredients:

1 1/2 cups uncooked quinoa, rinsed well

2 1/4 cups water

1/2 teaspoon vanilla

2 tablespoons pure maple syrup

Pinch of salt

1/4 teaspoon ground cinnamon

Optional toppings:

Milk, sliced almonds, fresh berries

Directions:

1. Combine quinoa, water, vanilla, maple syrup, salt and cinnamon in the Instant Pot.

2. Cover with lid and set the valve to "seal". Choose "Manual" and adjust to 1 minute cooking time at high pressure. At the end of the cooking time, use the 10-minute Natural Release.

3. Carefully open the lid and fluff the quinoa.

4. Serve with optional toppings.

Creamy Chocolate Steel Cut Oats (Clean eating)

You can make this ahead if your morning will be busy.

Preparation time: 2 minutes

Cooking time: 10 minutes

Servings: 8

Ingredients:

2 cups steel cut oats

1/2 cup of sugar or sweetener of choice

2 tablespoons unsweetened cocoa powder

3 1/2 cups water

Directions:

1. Combine all the ingredients in the pressure cooker. Stir well.

2. Cover with lid and set the valve to "seal". Choose "Manual" and adjust to 15 minutes cooking time at high pressure. Release the pressure with quick release.

Eggs With Herbs de Provence (Gluten Free)

Preparation time: 5 minutes

Cooking time: 20 minutes

Servings: 4

Ingredients:

6 eggs

1/2 cup heavy cream

1 cup cooked ham or bacon

1 small onion chopped

1 cup cheddar cheese

1 teaspoon Herbs de Provence

1 cup chopped kale leaves

1/8 teaspoon sea salt

1/8 teaspoon pepper

Directions:

1. In a bowl, combine eggs and heavy cream then whisk together.

2. Whisk in the other ingredients. Pour the mixture into a casserole dish that can fit into the Instant Pot. Cover the dish.

3. Fit the trivet into the Instant Pot and place the casserole dish on it.

4. Cover with lid and set the valve to "seal". Choose "Manual" and adjust to 20 minutes cooking time at high pressure. At the end of the cooking time, allow the pressure to release naturally.

5. Serve immediately.

Poached Eggs And Potato Hash (Gluten Free)

Preparation time: 5 minutes

Cooking time: 10 minutes

Servings: 2

Ingredients:

1 cup of peeled, cubed potatoes

2 tablespoons bacon fat

1 medium onion, diced

2 eggs

1 tablespoons cooked, chopped bacon

1 teaspoon Gluten Free Taco Seasoning, plus more

1 jalapeno pepper, sliced

1 tablespoon cilantro, plus more

Directions:

1. Pour 1 cup of water into the Instant Pot then fit the trivet inside.

2. Add the potato cubes to a casserole dish that can fit into the Instant Pot. Place the casserole dish on the trivet.

3. Cover with lid and set the valve to "seal". Choose "Manual" and adjust to 2 minutes cooking time at high pressure. At the end of the cooking time, use the quick release method to release the pressure.

4. Remove the potatoes and set aside. Remove the trivet then drain the water.

5. Set the Instant Pot to "sauté" and add the bacon fat. When hot, add the onions and cook with frequent stirring until tender, about 5 minutes.

6. Return the potatoes, to the pot then stir in bacon, Taco Seasoning, jalapeno pepper and cilantro.

7. Use a spoon to create a crater in the middle of the potatoes. Crack the two eggs gently into the center.

8. Cover with lid and set the valve to "seal". Choose "Manual" and adjust to 1 minute cooking time at high pressure. Again, use the quick release method to release the pressure.

9. Use a flat wooden spatula to carefully lift the potato hash with the eggs unto a serving platter. Be careful not to break the egg yolk.

10. Sprinkle with taco seasoning and cilantro then serve.

Vegetable Breakfast (Clean eating)

Preparation time: 25 minutes

Cooking time: 8 minutes

Servings: 4

Ingredients:

1 tablespoon olive oil

1 small sweet onion, peeled, diced

2 medium potatoes, peeled, diced

2 large carrots, peeled, diced

1 large red bell pepper, seeded, diced

1 stalk celery, diced

1/4 cup water

1 tablespoon low-sodium soy sauce

2 medium tomatoes, peeled, diced

1 cup zucchini, peeled, diced

Freshly ground black pepper, to taste

Directions:

1. Set the Instant Pot to "sauté" and add the oil. Add onion then sauté for about 2 minutes.

2. Stir in the potatoes, carrots, bell pepper and celery. Cook for 2 minutes then add water and soy sauce.

3. Cover with lid and set the valve to "seal". Choose "Manual" and adjust to 2 minutes cooking time at high pressure. At the end of the cooking time, use the quick release method to release the pressure.

4. Open the lid and stir in tomatoes and zucchini. Cover again with lid and set the valve to "seal". Choose "Manual" and adjust to 1 minute cooking time at high pressure. Again, use the quick release method to release the pressure.

5. Open the lid, add pepper to taste and adjust seasonings as necessary.

6. Serve as filling for sandwich wraps or simply over rice.

Oatmeal Couscous And Vegetable Porridge (Clean Eating)

This combination of oatmeal and vegetables is a breakfast delight.

Preparation time: 5 minutes

Cooking time: 5 minutes

Servings: 4

Ingredients:

2 tablespoons butter

1 small yellow onion, diced

4 carrots, diced finely

3 cups water

2 cups milk

1 cup rolled oats

1 cup couscous

1/2 teaspoon cinnamon

1 teaspoon sea salt

Directions:

1. Press "sauté" and melt butter in the Instant Pot. Add the onion then sauté for 1 minute.

2. Add carrots, water, milk, oats, couscous, cinnamon and salt. Stir well.

3. Cover with lid and set the valve to "seal". Choose "Manual" and adjust to 5 minutes cooking time at high pressure. At the end of the cooking time, use the 10-minute Natural Release.

4. Open the lid, fluff and serve.

Sausage Links And Corn Breakfast (Clean eating)

Preparation time: 10 minutes

Cooking time: 12 minutes

Servings: 4

Ingredients:

1 pound of pork sausage links

4 large potatoes, peeled, thinly sliced

1 medium sweet onion, peeled, diced

1 (16-ounce) can of creamed corn

1/4 teaspoon pepper

3/4 cup of tomato juice

Salt, to taste

Directions:

1. Select the "sauté" on your Instant Pot and add the sausage links. Brown sausage links then transfer to a plate.

2. To the Instant Pot, Add potatoes, top with onions then add the corn. Season with pepper then place sausage links on top. Lastly, pour in the tomato juice.

3. Cover with lid and set the valve to "seal". Choose "Manual" and adjust to 7 minutes cooking time at high pressure. At the end of the cooking time, allow the pressure to release naturally.

4. Taste and adjust seasoning as necessary.

Cheesy Sausage Scramble (Clean eating)

This goes well with toasted whole grain bread.

Preparation time: 20 minutes

Cooking time: 27 minutes

Servings: 8

Ingredients:

1 tablespoon vegetable oil

1 large sweet onion, diced

1 yellow bell pepper, seeded, diced

1 red bell pepper, seeded, diced

1 green bell pepper, seeded, diced

1 (1-pound) bag frozen hash browns, thawed

1 pound ground sausage

8 large eggs

1/4 cup water

Salt, to taste

Freshly ground pepper, to taste

1/2 pound grated Cheddar cheese

Directions:

1. Press "sauté" and heat oil in the Instant Pot. Add onion and bell peppers. Cook and stir for 5 minutes, or until onion is translucent. Stir in the hash browns and sausage.

2. Cover with lid and set the valve to "seal". Choose "Manual" and adjust to 10 minutes cooking time at Low pressure. At the end of the cooking time, use the quick release method to release the pressure.

3. Open the lid carefully, then drain any excess fat. Return the Instant Pot to "sauté".

4. Whisk together eggs, water, salt and pepper. Pour over the potato-sausage mixture in the Instant Pot. Stir and scramble the eggs until they start to set.

5. Stir in the cheese and continue scrambling until eggs are done and the cheese has melted.

6. Serve immediately.

Fruity Irish Oatmeal (Clean eating)

If you want different flavors, substitute other dried fruit like cherries, dates and prunes.

Preparation time: 5 minutes

Cooking time: 8 minutes

Servings: 2

Ingredients:

3 cups of water, divided

1 cup toasted steel-cut oats

1 cup apple juice

2 teaspoons butter

1 tablespoon maple syrup

1 tablespoon snipped dried apricots

1 tablespoon golden raisins

1 tablespoon dried cranberries

1/4 teaspoon ground cinnamon

1 pinch salt

To serve:

Maple syrup, chopped toasted nuts (pecans, walnuts), milk

Directions:

1. Place the trivet in the Instant Pot then pour in 1/2 cup of water.

2. In a metal bowl that can fit in the Instant Pot, combine oats, 2 1/2 cups water, apple juice, butter, maple syrup, apricots, raisins, cranberries, cinnamon and salt. Stir well to combine, then place the bowl on the trivet.

3. Cover with lid and set the valve to "seal". Choose "Manual" and adjust to 8 minutes cooking time at Low pressure. At the end of the cooking time, allow the pressure to release naturally.

4. Using tongs, remove the metal bowl from the Instant Pot.

5. Spoon into bowls and top with maple syrup, chopped toasted nuts (pecans, walnuts) and milk.

SOUPS, STEWS, AND CHILIES

Red Cabbage Chicken Soup (Paleo)

Not only does this soup have bold flavors, it is also highly nourishing.

Preparation time: 25 minutes

Cooking time: 40 minutes

Servings: 4

Ingredients:

2 large carrots, cubed

1 medium chicken, cleaned, trussed

½ medium red cabbage, cored, cubed

2 garlic cloves, smashed

1 red onion, cut into wedges

1 teaspoon white peppercorns (omit for AIP)

Water

1-2 tablespoons tamarind paste

1 teaspoon ginger powder

1 teaspoon cinnamon powder

1 teaspoon turmeric powder

½ pineapple, cut into small chunks

1 lime

Sea salt, to taste

Fish sauce, to taste

2 spring onions, sliced finely

Directions:

1. Arrange the carrots on the bottom of the inner pot.

2. Next, add the chicken, red cabbage, garlic, red onion and peppercorns. Pour in enough water to cover all the ingredients.

3. Cover with lid and set the valve to "sealing". Select "soup" setting for 25-30 minutes at high pressure.

4. At the end of the cooking time, use the 10-minute Natural Release to release the pressure.

5. In a small bowl, combine about 1/2 cup of the cooking liquid with the tamarind paste.

6. Remove the chicken and use 2 forks to shred the meat. Return the meat to cooking liquid in the pot.

7. Mix the tamarind paste to form a thickened paste then gently squeeze to remove the pods. Stir the thickened paste into the pot.

8. Stir in the ginger, cinnamon and turmeric. Gently stir in the pineapple chunks.

9. Squeeze in half of the lime and cut the remaining half into 4 wedges.

10. Select the "Sauté" setting and cook for 5-10 minutes.

11. Add sea salt and fish sauce to taste. Serve, garnished with slices of spring onions and lime wedges.

Mixed Vegetable Chicken Soup (Paleo, AIP)
Enjoy this soup and get a healthy serving of veggies at the same time.

Preparation time: 5 minutes

Cooking time: 30 minutes

Servings: 4

Ingredients:

4 large chicken drumsticks

2 medium carrots, peeled, diced

2 large ribs celery, sliced

1 medium rutabaga, peeled, diced

1 large parsnip, peeled, diced

½ teaspoon cracked black pepper (omit for AIP)

1 small yellow onion, diced

2 bay leaves

4 cups low sodium chicken broth

Directions:

1. Add all the ingredients to the pot and pour in the chicken broth.

2. Cover with lid and set the valve to "seal". Choose "Soup" and adjust to 30 minutes cooking time at high pressure.

3. At the end of the cooking time, allow the pressure to release naturally.

4. Open the cover and use a slotted spoon to remove the drumsticks. Set aside to cool.

5. Strip the meat from the bones and discard the bones and skin. Return meat to the cooking liquid in the pot and stir. Serve in bowls.

Beef And Potato Stew (Clean eating)

Preparation time: 20 minutes

Cooking time: 55 minutes

Servings: 8

Ingredients:

3 pounds stew beef chuck roast, cubed

1/2 teaspoon salt

1/2 teaspoon black pepper

2 tablespoons ghee

1/2 onion, diced

2 tablespoons tomato paste

2 garlic cloves, minced

3 cups beef broth

3/4 cup red wine

1/2 teaspoon dried thyme

3 celery stalks, cut into chunks

3 parsnips, peeled, cut into chunks

3 carrots, peeled, cut into chunks

1 1/2 pounds red or golden potatoes, cut into chunks

Salt and pepper to taste

1 small handful parsley, chopped

Directions:

1. In a bowl, toss the beef with salt and pepper.

2. Add the ghee to the Instant Pot and press "Sauté". When fat has melted, add the beef in batches and brown on each side for 3 minutes. Set browned beef aside in a plate.

3. Add onion and cook until tender, about 4 minutes. Add tomato paste and garlic; cook for just 30 seconds.

4. Add the broth and wine, bring to a simmer and scrape up any browned bits.

5. Return the beef, along with any accumulated juices to the pot. Add thyme, celery, parsnips, carrots and potatoes.

6. Cover with lid and set the valve to "seal". Choose "Meat/Stew" and adjust to 20 minutes cooking time at high pressure. At the end of the cooking time, allow the pressure to release naturally.

7. Open the lid and gently remove the solid vegetables from the pot. Press the "Sauté" button again and cook for about 10 minutes, or until thickened.

8. Taste and add salt and pepper as necessary. Return the vegetables to the pot, stir in the chopped parsley and serve.

Instant Pot Lamb Stew (Paleo, AIP)

This meal is made for those days when you just want to throw everything into a pot and come back to eat.

Preparation time: 10 minutes

Cooking time: 36 minutes

Servings: 4-5

Ingredients:

1 acorn squash

2 pounds lamb stew meat, cubed

1 large yellow onion, peeled, sliced

3 large carrots, sliced

6 garlic cloves, sliced

2 sprigs rosemary

1 bay leaf

3 tablespoon broth

1/2 teaspoon salt, or to taste

Directions:

1. Microwave the acorn squash for 1 minute then peel it, remove the seeds and cut it into cubes.

2. Combine all the ingredients in the Instant Pot. Cover with lid and set the valve to "seal". Choose "Soup/Stew" and cook for 35 minutes at high pressure.

3. At the end of the cooking time, allow the pressure to release naturally. Carefully open the lid and serve.

Spicy Corn Chowder (Clean eating)

Preparation time: 15 minutes

Cooking time: 10 minutes

Servings: 6

Ingredients:

2 tablespoons butter

4 large leeks, root ends cut off, bruised outer leaves discarded

2 cups water

4 cups chicken broth

6 medium russet potatoes, peeled, diced

2 (4-ounce) cans chopped green chili peppers, drained

1 bay leaf

Salt, to taste

Freshly ground black pepper, to taste

1 1/2 cups fresh or frozen corn

1/2 cup fat-free half-and-half

Pinch sugar

1/2 teaspoon dried thyme

Directions:

1. Melt butter in the Instant Pot, using the "sauté" function.

2. Slice the leeks and add to the Instant Pot. Sauté for 2 minutes.

3. Stir in water, broth, potatoes, green chili peppers and bay leaf. Season with salt and pepper.

4. Cover with lid and set the valve to "seal". Choose "Manual" and adjust to 4 minutes cooking time at high pressure. At the end of the cooking time, use the quick release method to release the pressure.

5. Open the lid, remove bay leaf and discard.

6. Stir in the corn, half-and-half, sugar and thyme. Press "sauté" and heat through with occasional stirring.

7. Serve with sandwiches.

Simple Potato Soup (Clean eating)
A healthy and familiar favorite, cooked very quickly in your Instant Pot.

Preparation time: 25 minutes

Cooking time: 6 minutes

Servings: 8

Ingredients:

2-3 tablespoons butter

3 garlic cloves, minced

1 package soft tofu

2 tablespoons lemon juice

1 cup almond milk

1 teaspoon dried dill

1/2 teaspoon salt

2 cups sliced mushrooms

4 cups diced potatoes

2 cups sliced onion

1 cup chopped celery

1 cup chopped carrot

4 cups of vegetable broth

Ground black pepper, to taste

Directions:

1. Press "sauté" and melt the butter in your Instant Pot. Add the garlic and cook for 1 minute.

2. In a food processor or blender, combine tofu, lemon juice, almond milk, dill and salt. Pulse until creamy.

3. To the Instant Pot, add mushrooms, potatoes, onion, celery, carrot and half of the broth. Pour in the tofu cream. Pour the remaining broth into the blender and pulse briefly to get out the remaining tofu cream. Pour into the Instant Pot.

4. Cover with lid and set the valve to "seal". Choose "Manual" and adjust to 5 minutes cooking time at high pressure. At the end of the cooking time, use the quick release method to release the pressure.

5. Serve with ground black pepper.

Spicy Chicken Chili (Clean eating)

Preparation time: 30 minutes

Cooking time: 45 minutes

Servings: 8

Ingredients:

1 cup dried pinto beans, soaked in water overnight

5 cups water

2 teaspoons canola oil

1 tablespoon olive oil

1 onion, peeled, diced

1 large carrot, peeled, diced

2 jalapeño peppers, seeded, diced

2 red bell peppers, seeded, diced

1 chipotle pepper, seeded, diced

4 (4-ounce) cans chopped green chili peppers

4 garlic cloves, peeled, minced

4 cups chicken broth

3 pounds meaty chicken pieces, skin removed

2 tablespoons all-purpose flour

2 tablespoons butter

Salt, to taste

Freshly ground black pepper, to taste

Directions:

1. Drain the pinto beans then add to the Instant Pot. Add 5 cups water and canola oil.

2. Cover with lid and set the valve to "seal". Choose "Manual" and adjust to 15 minutes cooking time at high pressure. At the end of the cooking time, allow the pressure to release naturally.

3. Strain the beans and set aside. Wash and dry the Instant Pot.

4. Add olive oil to the Instant Pot and press "sauté". When hot, sauté onion for 3 minutes. Add carrot and sauté for 3 minutes.

5. Stir in jalapeño and red bell peppers then sauté until soft, about 5 minutes.

6. Add the chipotle peppers, canned peppers, garlic, chicken broth and chicken pieces.

7. Cover with lid and set the valve to "seal". Choose "Manual" and adjust to 12 minutes cooking time at high pressure. At the end of the cooking time, use the quick release method to release the pressure.

8. Remove chicken pieces and place in a bowl. When cool enough, remove the meat from bones and return the meat to the Instant Pot.

9. Stir in the beans. Press "Sauté" and bring the sauce to a boil.

10. Make a paste with the flour and butter then whisk into the chili.

11. Let simmer for about 5 minutes, until the chili thickens. Taste and add salt and pepper as necessary.

12. Serve with tortilla chips or cornbread along with sour cream and cheddar cheese.

Easy Beef Stew (Paleo, AIP)

If you want a more filling meal, serve this stew over squash or mashed sweet potatoes.

Preparation time: 15 minutes

Cooking time: 1 hour 5 minutes

Servings: 6-8

Ingredients:

2 tablespoons solid fat (lard or bacon drippings)

2 pounds grass-fed beef stew meat

4 strips bacon, sliced

2 1/2 cups chopped scallion greens

2 1/2 cups cubed rutabaga

2 1/2 cups chopped carrots

2 tablespoons fresh parsley

2 tablespoons fresh thyme leaves

1.5 cup red wine

1.5 cup bone broth

2 dried bay leaves

2 teaspoons salt, or to taste

Directions:

1. Add the fat to the Instant Pot and melt with the "Sauté" function. Pat the meat dry with paper towels.

2. Working in batches, brown the meat on all sides. Remove browned beef and set aside.

3. Add the bacon, and scallion greens. Sauté, stirring occasionally, until bacon is crisp and scallions are just tender.

4. Return the browned beef to the pot then add the rutabaga, carrots, parsley, thyme, wine and broth. Season with salt, stir everything together then push in the bay leaves

5. Cover with lid and set the valve to "seal". Choose "Manual" and adjust to 50 minutes cooking time at high pressure. At the end of the cooking time, allow the pressure to release naturally.

6. Serve on its own or serve over squash or mashed sweet potatoes. Leftovers can be refrigerated.

Flavorful Beef Stew (Paleo)

This stew has a really nice flavor because the Instant Pot traps the flavors of the ingredients within the liquid.

Preparation time: 15 minutes

Cooking time: 55 minutes

Servings: 4

Ingredients:

2 1/2 pounds chuck roast, cubed

3 tablespoons vegetable oil

1 teaspoon kosher salt

2 cups chicken stock

1 teaspoon smoked paprika

16 ounces tomato sauce

1/2 teaspoon garlic powder

2 large onions, sliced

1 pound carrots, cut into chunks

1 pound potatoes, cut into chunks

Directions:

1. Add oil to the Instant Pot then press the "Sauté" function. Salt the pieces of roast then brown in hot oil.

2. Return browned meat to pot then add chicken stock, smoked paprika and tomato sauce.

3. Cover with lid and set the valve to "seal". Choose "Soup" and adjust to 15 minutes cooking time at high pressure. At the end of the cooking time, use the quick release method to release the pressure.

4. Open the pot and add garlic powder, onions, carrots and potatoes.

5. Cover with lid and set the valve to "seal". Choose "Soup" again and adjust to 30 minutes cooking time at high pressure. Enjoy.

Chicken Tortilla Soup (Clean eating) .

Preparation time: 10 minutes

Cooking time: 20 minutes

Servings: 4

Ingredients:

1 tablespoon olive oil

1 medium onion, chopped

2 garlic cloves, minced

2 tablespoon fresh cilantro, chopped

2 (6-inch) corn tortillas, chopped into 1-inch squares

1 cup frozen corn

1 (15-ounce) can black beans

3 chicken breasts

1 very large ripe tomato, chopped

3-4 cups chicken broth

1/4 teaspoon ground cayenne pepper

1 teaspoon ground cumin

2 teaspoon chili powder

1 bay leaf

To serve:

Vegetable oil for frying

Corn tortillas, sliced into strips

Fresh cilantro

Fresh lime juice

Grated cheese

Directions:

1. Set the Instant Pot to "Sauté" and add the olive oil. When hot, add the onions and cook with frequent stirring until tender, about 5 minutes.

2. Stir in the garlic, cilantro and tortilla squares. Cook for 1 minute more.

3. Add the corn, black beans, chicken, tomato, 3 cups broth, cayenne pepper, cumin, chili powder and bay leaf. Cancel the "Sauté" function.

4. Cover with lid and set the valve to "seal". Choose "Soup" and adjust to 4 minutes cooking time at high pressure.

5. Meanwhile, start preparing the toppings. Add the vegetable oil to a medium-sized skillet and heat on medium heat. Fry tortilla strips, until golden on both sides. Transfer to paper towel lined plate to drain. Salt tortillas lightly.

6. Slice the lime wedges, chop the cilantro and grate the cheese.

7. At the end of the cooking time, use the quick release method to release the pressure. Remove chicken and shred with two forks. Return shredded chicken to the Instant Pot and stir with the contents.

8. Serve the soup in bowls along with crisp tortilla strips, cilantro, shredded cheese and lime juice.

Easy Pork Stew (Paleo)

This is as easy as the name goes, yet gives the feeling of eating wonderful home cooking.

Preparation time: 10 minutes

Cooking time: 40 minutes

Servings: 6

Ingredients:

3 pounds boneless pork ham, diced

2 onions chopped, peeled, chopped

1 can whole mushrooms, drained

3 large carrots, peeled, sliced

2 cups of beef broth

2 bay leaves

Salt and pepper, to taste

Ghee

Directions:

1. Season the diced pork with salt and pepper.

2. Add ghee to the Instant Pot and press "Sauté". When fat has melted, add the diced pork in batches and brown on each side for about 2 minutes. Set browned pork aside in a plate.

3. Add the onions, mushrooms and carrots to the pot, adding more ghee if necessary. Cook and stir for a few minutes. Remove and set aside.

4. Return browned pork to the Instant Pot, pour in the broth then add the bay leaves.

5. Cover with lid and set the valve to "seal". Choose "Meat/Stew" and adjust to 30-35 minutes cooking time at high pressure. At the end of the cooking time, use the quick release method to release the pressure.

6. Return the onions, mushrooms and carrots to the pot.

7. Cover with lid and set the valve to "seal". Choose "Manual" and adjust to 3 minutes cooking time at high pressure. Again, use the quick release method to release the pressure.

Beef And Vegetable Soup (Paleo, AIP)

Preparation time: 15 minutes

Cooking time: 1 hour

Servings: 4-6

Ingredients:

1 1/2 pounds beef shank

2 tablespoons extra virgin olive oil divided

1 tablespoon apple cider vinegar

8 cups filtered water

3 garlic cloves, peeled

2 sprigs of fresh thyme

1 teaspoon salt

2 bay leaves

1 onion, finely chopped

4 medium carrots, chopped

2 celery stalks, chopped

1 parsnip, chopped

1 1/2 cups turnip, chopped

½ teaspoon dried marjoram

½ teaspoon dried thyme

2 cups cabbage, chopped

¼ cup of fresh parsley (optional for garnish)

Directions:

1. Add 1 tablespoon oil to the Instant Pot and select the "Sauté" function. Brown the shank about 2 minutes per side.

2. Add apple cider vinegar, water, garlic cloves, thyme, salt and bay leaves.

3. Cover with lid and set the valve to "seal". Choose "Manual" and adjust to 45 minutes cooking time at high pressure. At the end of the cooking time, use the quick release method to release the pressure.

4. Remove the lid the strain the broth into a bowl, discarding the thyme sprigs, garlic and bay leaves. Transfer the meat to a cutting board, shred and remove the fat.

5. Add another 1 tablespoon of oil and select the "Sauté" function again. Add onions, carrots, celery, parsnip and turnip. Cook for about 3 minutes.

6. Stir in the marjoram and thyme then cancel the "Sauté" function.

7. Return the broth and shredded meat to the pot, along with the cabbage. Cover with lid and set the valve to "seal". Choose "Manual" and adjust to 4 minutes cooking time at high pressure. At the end of the cooking time, allow the pressure to release naturally.

8. Remove the lid and serve, garnished with parsley if you like.

POULTRY MAIN DISHES

Turkey And Gravy (Paleo, AIP)
Get this deliciously flavored dish on your table in just 75 minutes.

Preparation time: 15 minutes

Cooking time: 60 minutes

Servings: 6

Ingredients:

1 (4-5 pound) bone-in, skin-on turkey breast

Salt, to taste

Black pepper, to taste (omit for AIP)

2 coconut oil

1 medium onion, diced

1 celery rib, diced

1 large carrot, diced

2 teaspoons dried sage

1 garlic clove, peeled, crushed

¼ cup dry white wine

1½ cups of bone broth (chicken or turkey)

1 bay leaf

Directions:

1. Pat the turkey dry and rub all over with salt and pepper (omit pepper for AIP).

2. Heat coconut oil in the Instant Pot, using the "sauté" function. Add the turkey breast with skin side down. Brown for about 5 minutes. Remove turkey and set aside in a plate, leaving the fat in pot.

3. Add onion, celery and carrot to pot, choose "sauté" and cook for about 5 minutes. Remove vegetables and set aside in a plate, leaving the fat in pot.

4. Stir in sage and garlic and cook for just 30 seconds. Add the wine and cook until reduced slightly, about 3 minutes.

5. Add broth and bay leaf. Stir with a wooden spoon, scraping any browned bits stuck to bottom of pot.

6. Add the turkey with skin side up, along with any accumulated juices.

7. Cover with lid and set the valve to "sealing". Select "poultry" setting for 35 minutes at high pressure.

8. Use quick release method and remove lid carefully. Transfer the turkey breast to a carving board and cover loosely with foil.

9. Transfer the cooking liquid to a regular blender or use an immersion blender to blend until smooth.

10. Return to the Instant Pot and select the "sauté" function. Cook until reduce to about 2 cups. Taste and adjust seasoning if necessary.

11. Slice the turkey breast and serve it with hot gravy.

Chicken With Sauerkraut And Cranberries Sauce (Paleo, AIP)

Simply combine the ingredients and let the Instant Pot do its job.

Preparation time: 10 minutes

Cooking time: 25 minutes

Servings: 6-8

Ingredients:

2 cups of sauerkraut, drained

3 garlic cloves, peeled, crushed, chopped roughly

¼ cup raisins

3-4 pounds chicken thighs

1 small preserved lemon, chopped, seeded

1 1/2 cups frozen or fresh cranberries, divided

1 teaspoon dried thyme

½ tablespoon dried parsley flakes

1 teaspoon ground cinnamon

1 cup apple cider (non-alcoholic)

1 teaspoon sea salt

1 teaspoon arrowroot flour

2 teaspoon water

Directions:

1. Add sauerkraut then scatter garlic and raisins over evenly.

2. Add the chicken to the pot, sprinkle over with the preserved lemon and 1 cup of cranberries.

3. In a small bowl, mix together thyme, parsley flakes, cinnamon, apple cider and sea salt. Pour the mixture into the pot.

4. Cover with lid and set the valve to "sealing". Select "poultry" setting for 25-30 minutes at high pressure.

5. At the end of the cooking time, release the pressure naturally.

6. Remove chicken pieces from the pot and place in a deep oven dish. Broil for about 5 minutes until browned.

7. Select the "sauté" setting on the Instant Pot, add the remaining ½ cup of cranberries.

8. Mix arrowroot flour with a little water to make slurry. Stir it into the sauce.

9. Let the sauce simmer until thickened then turn off the Instant Pot.

10. Serve chicken with the sauerkraut and cranberry sauce.

Instant Pot Whole Chicken (Paleo, AIP)

With your Instant Pot, you can cook a whole chicken quickly and easily.

Preparation time: 5 minutes

Cooking time: 25 minutes

Servings: 4-6

Ingredients:

1 whole chicken (3-4 pounds)

1 tablespoon coconut oil

Salt

Pepper (omit for AIP)

1 cup water

Directions:

1. Heat oil in the Instant Pot, using the "sauté" function. Season chicken with salt and pepper then brown on each side for just 1 minute.

2. Remove the chicken, fit the steam rack inside the pot and pour water into the pot. Place the chicken on the steam rack.

3. Cover and lock the lid. Set the Instant Pot to "poultry" on high pressure and adjust the time to 25-30 minutes (depending on the size of chicken).

4. At the end of the cooking time, let the pressure release naturally for about 15 minutes.

5. Remove the chicken and shred.

Sweet And Sour Mango Chicken (Paleo, AIP)

A delicious mix of flavors that is thoroughly pleasing.

Preparation time: 10 minutes

Cooking time: 40 minutes

Servings: 4

Ingredients:

1 tablespoon cooking fat (bacon fat or lard)

8 chicken thighs, boneless

1/2 red onion, chopped

4 garlic cloves, chopped

1 mango, cut into 1/2 inch chunks

1/4 cup + 1 tablespoon coconut aminos, divided

2 tablespoons apple cider vinegar, divided

Juice of 1 lime

1/4 cup chopped cilantro

1 inch piece of ginger, finely chopped

1/2 cup chicken broth

2 tablespoons honey

1 teaspoon fish sauce

1/2 teaspoon salt

1 green onion, green part only, sliced

Directions:

1. Preheat the Instant Pot by pressing the "sauté" function, add the cooking fat and heat until melted.

2. Add the chicken thighs with face down (you may have to work in batches). Brown for about 3 minutes, flip over and brown on the other side for 3 minutes. Remove browned chicken and set aside.

3. Add the onion, garlic and mango to the pot. Cook until onions are translucent and mango is light brown.

4. Press the cancel button then return the chicken to the pot.

5. Add 1/4 cup coconut aminos, 1 tablespoon apple cider vinegar, lime juice, cilantro, ginger, chicken broth, honey, fish sauce and salt.

6. Cover with lid and set the valve to "seal". Choose "Poultry" and 15 minutes cooking time at high pressure. At the end of the cooking time, use the quick release method to release the pressure.

7. Open the lid and transfer the chicken to a serving platter.

8. Select the "sauté" function and cook the sauce until thickened, about 10-15 minutes.

9. Serve chicken thighs with sauce poured over and garnished with green onion slices.

BBQ Chicken (Paleo)

This delicious BBQ chicken is perfect for weeknight meals on busy days.

Preparation time: 5 minutes

Cooking time: 20 minutes

Servings: 4

Ingredients:

1 pound boneless skinless chicken breasts

1 cup water

1 tablespoon apple cider vinegar

1/2 cup Paleo barbecue sauce

Directions:

1. In a small bowl, combine water, apple cider vinegar and barbecue sauce.

2. Add chicken to the inner pot of the Instant Pot, Pour the sauce over.

3. Cover with lid and set the valve to "seal". Choose "Poultry" and adjust to 20 minutes cooking time at high pressure.

4. At the end of the cooking time, use the quick release method to release the pressure.

5. Open the lid, remove the chicken and shred with two forks.

6. If you want to thicken the sauce, use the "sauté" function for a few minutes.

7. Return shredded chicken to the pot and toss with the sauce. Serve.

Sweet Apple Chicken And Cabbage (Paleo)

The simplicity of this dish makes dinner easy when times are busy.

Preparation time: 5 minutes

Cooking time: 30 minutes

Servings: 4

Ingredients:

1 small head cabbage, cored, shredded

2 pounds boneless, skinless chicken breasts

1 cup frozen or fresh cranberries

2 apples, cored, sliced

1/2 cup chicken broth

1 tablespoon maple syrup

1 tablespoon apple cider vinegar

1 teaspoon ground ginger

1 teaspoon cinnamon

1/2 teaspoon salt, or to taste

Directions:

1. In the Instant Pot, layer the shredded cabbage, followed by the chicken then place apples and cranberries on top of chicken.

2. Pour in the broth then add maple syrup, apple cider vinegar, ginger, cinnamon and salt.

3. Cover with lid and set the valve to "seal". Choose "Poultry" and adjust to 20 minutes cooking time at high pressure. At the end of the cooking time, use the 10-minute Natural Release.

4. Open the lid and serve.

Chicken Fennel Soup (Paleo, AIP)

Make this when you are in need of serious nourishment.

Preparation time: 20 minutes

Cooking time: 30 minutes

Servings: 6-8

Ingredients:

1 large bulb of fennel, chopped

1 pound skinless, boneless chicken breast, cut into bite size pieces

1/2 onion, chopped

4 green onions, chopped

3 garlic cloves, peeled, chopped

1 cup chopped spinach or kale

4 cups filtered water

2 cups chicken or bone broth

1 tablespoon dried oregano

1 bay leaf

1/8 teaspoon salt

Directions:

1. Combine all the ingredients in the Instant Pot.

2. Cover with lid and set the valve to "seal". Choose "Soup" and adjust to 30 minutes cooking time at high pressure.

3. At the end of the cooking time, use the 10-minute Natural Release.

4. Open the lid and serve.

Sweet Tropical Chicken (Paleo, AIP)

This will remind you of the colors and flavors of the tropics.

Preparation time: 15 minutes

Cooking time: 15 minutes

Servings: 4

Ingredients:

2 pounds chicken thighs, cut into bite size pieces

1/2 cup full fat coconut cream

1 cup pineapple chunks, fresh or frozen

2 tablespoons coconut aminos

1 teaspoon cinnamon

1/8 teaspoon salt

1/2 cup chopped green onion (for garnish)

Directions:

1. In the Instant Pot, combine all the ingredients except green onions.

2. Cover with lid and set the valve to "seal". Choose "Poultry" and cook at 15 minutes at high pressure. At the end of the cooking time, use the 10-minute Natural Release.

3. Open the lid and stir the sauce. If you want a thicker sauce, press the "sauté" function and cook for a few minutes more.

4. Serve with chopped green onions.

Honey Dijon Chicken (Paleo)

Weeknight meals don't come easier than this recipe.

Preparation time: 5 minutes

Cooking time: 20 minutes

Servings: 4

Ingredients:

1 pound boneless skinless chicken breasts

1 cup water

1/4 cup honey

1/4 cup whole grain mustard

Paleo hot sauce, to taste

Directions:

1. In a small bowl, combine water, honey, mustard and hot sauce.

2. Add chicken to the inner pot of the Instant Pot and pour the sauce over.

3. Cover with lid and set the valve to "seal". Choose "Poultry" and adjust to 20 minutes cooking time at high pressure.

4. At the end of the cooking time, use the quick release method to release the pressure.

5. Open the lid, remove the chicken and shred with two forks.

6. If you want to thicken the sauce, use the "sauté" function for a few minutes.

7. Return shredded chicken to the pot and toss with the sauce. Serve.

Texas Turkey Chili (Clean Eating)

Preparation time: 10 minutes

Cooking time: 20 minutes

Servings: 8

Ingredients:

2 tablespoons canola oil, or preferred frying oil

1 large onion, peeled, chopped

1 1/2 pounds of ground turkey

2 cups homemade Bloody Mary mix

2 (14-ounce) cans kidney beans, drained, rinsed

2 (14-ounce) cans diced tomatoes with green chilies

1 1/2 cups water

4 tablespoons chili powder, divided

Directions:

1. Heat oil in the Instant Pot, using the "sauté" function.

2. Add the onion and cook, until light golden, about 7 minutes.

3. Add the ground turkey. Cook until brown, stirring and breaking it up in the process.

4. Add the Bloody Mary then stir well and scrape up any browned bits from the bottom of the pot.

5. Stir in the beans, tomatoes, 2 tablespoons of chili powder and the water. Bring to boil.

6. Cover with lid and set the valve to "seal". Choose "Manual" and adjust to 5 minutes cooking time at high pressure. At the end of the cooking time, use the quick release method to release the pressure.

7. Open the lid carefully and stir in 2 tablespoons of chili powder then let sit for about 5 minutes before serving. Serve with your desired side and garnish.

Braised Turkey Thighs (Clean Eating)

Preparation time: 15 minutes

Cooking time: 1 hour 20 minutes

Servings: 4

Ingredients:

2 turkey thighs, fat trimmed

1 cup chicken broth

1 tablespoon red-wine vinegar

1 large onion, thinly sliced

2 teaspoon minced garlic

1 cup sliced Portobello mushrooms

1/2 teaspoon dried thyme

1/2 teaspoon dried sage

1/2 teaspoon dried rosemary

1/2 teaspoon each salt and pepper

3 tablespoons flour

1/4 cup water

Directions:

1. Using the "sauté" function, heat a little oil in the Instant Pot. Brown the turkey thighs for a few minutes then add the other ingredients, except flour and water.

2. Cover with lid and set the valve to "seal". Choose "Poultry" and adjust to 1 hour cooking time at high pressure. At the end of the cooking time, use the quick release method to release the pressure. Check for doneness, and if necessary, cook for about 10 minutes more under Poultry setting.

3. Transfer the turkey to a cutting board and cover with foil loosely.

4. In a small bowl, whisk the flour and water together until smooth. Whisk the mixture into the cooking liquid in the Instant Pot.

5. Press "sauté", bring to a boil then press "Keep-warm" and allow to simmer gently for 15 minutes.

6. Cut the turkey meat and divide among 4 plates. Spoon the gravy over.

Duck And Vegetables (Clean eating)

A stress-free way to prepare delicious duck for dinner.

Preparation time: 15 minutes

Cooking time: 40 minutes

Servings: 8

Ingredients:

1 medium size duck

2 carrots, sliced

1 cucumber, sliced

1 inch piece of ginger, finely chopped

2 cups water

1 tablespoon cooking wine

2 teaspoons salt

Directions:

1.This is a dump dinner, so simply dump everything in the Instant Pot.

2. Cover with lid and set the valve to "seal". Choose "Meat/Stew" at 40 minutes cooking time at high pressure. At the end of the cooking time, allow the pressure to release naturally.

BEEF AND LAMB MAIN DISHES

Easy Braised Short Ribs (Paleo, AIP)

Preparation time: 5 minutes

Cooking time: 45 minutes

Servings: 8

Ingredients:

4-5 pounds beef short ribs

Kosher salt

1 tablespoon bacon fat, or oil of choice

1 onion, quartered

3 garlic, cloves

Water

Directions:

1. Season ribs on all sides generously with salt.

2. Add bacon fat or oil to the Instant Pot then select the "Sauté" function. When hot, add the beef and brown on all sides.

3. Return browned meat to the pot. Add garlic and onion and about 2 inches of water.

4. Choose "Meat/Stew" and adjust to 35 minutes cooking time at high pressure.

5. At the end of the cooking time, allow the pressure to release naturally.

6. Pull meat from the bones and discard the bone. Strain the cooking liquid, season to taste, then serve with meat.

Spicy Beef And Plantain (Paleo, AIP)

Preparation time: 5 minutes

Cooking time: 55 minutes

Servings: 5-6

Ingredients:

2 pounds bottom blade pot roast, cubed

2 small onions, sliced thinly

1 tablespoon coconut oil

1 cup coconut milk

1 stick cinnamon

4 kaffir lime leaves

1 very ripe plantain, cut into 1 inch chunks

Sea salt, to taste

1 tablespoon coriander leaves, chopped

For the marinade:

2 teaspoons coconut oil

1 teaspoon turmeric powder

1 teaspoon ginger powder

1 teaspoon garlic powder

1 teaspoon sea salt

Directions:

1. In a small bowl, mix together the ingredients for the marinade. Add beef and let marinate for about 1 hour.

2. Add coconut oil to the Instant Pot and choose the "Sauté" function. When hot, add the onion and cook until translucent. Remove onions and set aside.

3. Remove meat from marinade and brown on all sides in the hot oil, working in batches. Add more oil if necessary. Remove browned meat and set aside.

4. Stir the coconut milk into the pot, scraping any browned bits from the bottom of the pot. Add the browned meat, onions, cinnamon stick and kaffir lime leaves.

5. Cover with lid and set the valve to "seal". Choose "Manual" and cook for 35 minutes at high pressure. At the end of the cooking time, use the 10-minute Natural Release.

6. Open the pot, select "Sauté" and gently stir in the plantain. Season with sea salt and let simmer until the gravy is slightly thickened and plantain is cooked, about 5-7 minutes.

7. Remove and discard kaffir lime leaves and cinnamon stick. Serve sprinkled with chopped coriander.

Spicy Cranberry Pot Roast (Paleo, AIP)

Easy, fast, delicious and full of extra nutritional goodness!

Preparation time: 10 minutes

Cooking time: 2 hours

Servings: 4-6

Ingredients:

3-4 pounds beef arm roast

Salt and pepper (omit pepper for AIP)

2 tablespoons olive oil

2 1/2 cups bone broth

1 cup whole cranberries, frozen or fresh

¼ cup honey

½ cup water

3 inches cinnamon stick

1 teaspoon horseradish powder

6 whole cloves (omit for AIP)

2 large garlic cloves, peeled

Directions:

1. Pat the roast dry with paper towels and rub all over with salt and pepper.

2. Add oil to the Instant Pot and select the "sauté" function. When hot, brown meat on all sides, about 8-10 minutes. Remove browned meat and set aside.

3. Add about 1/2 cup of broth to the pot, stir and scrape up brown bits. Let simmer for 4-5 minutes with constant stirring.

4. Add the cranberries, honey, water, cinnamon stick, horseradish powder, cloves and garlic. Cook and stir for about 5 minutes, or until cranberries begin to burst.

5. Return the meat to the pot and add the remaining broth. Cover with lid and set the valve to "seal". Choose "Manual" and adjust to 75 minutes cooking time at high pressure.

6. At the end of the cooking time, allow the pressure to release naturally.

7. Transfer the meat to a serving platter. Serve with cooking juices.

Beef Bourguignon (Paleo, AIP)
Hearty and juicy beef in a delicious red wine sauce.

Preparation time: 20 minutes

Cooking time: 50 minutes

Servings: 4

Ingredients:

1 pound flank steak or stewing steak

1/2 pound bacon, sliced thinly

5 medium carrots, cut into sticks

1 large red onion, peeled, sliced

2 garlic cloves, minced

2 teaspoon rock salt

2 tablespoons dried thyme

2 tablespoons dried parsley

2 teaspoon ground black pepper (omit for AIP)

1 cup red wine

1/2 cup beef broth/stock

1 tablespoon olive oil or avocado oil

2 large sweet potato, peeled, cubed

1 tablespoon maple syrup

Directions:

1. Select the "sauté" function on your Instant Pot then add the oil.

2. Pat beef dry with paper towels and rub with salt and pepper then brown in the hot oil. Remove browned meat and set aside.

3. Add the bacon strips and onion. Cook until brown.

4. Return the beef to the pot then add all remaining ingredients.

5. Choose "Manual" and adjust to 30 minutes cooking time at high pressure. At the end of the cooking time, allow the pressure to release naturally.

Garlicky Teriyaki Beef (Paleo, AIP)

A lovely combination of the sweet taste of Teriyaki with flank steak.

Preparation time: 10 minutes

Cooking time: 45 minutes

Servings: 6

Ingredients:

12 pounds flank steak, cut into 1/2-inch strips

2 garlic cloves, chopped finely

Teriyaki sauce:

1/4 cup coconut aminos

2 tablespoons fish sauce

1/4 cup maple syrup

1 1/2 teaspoon ground ginger

1 tablespoon raw honey

Directions:

1. In the Instant Pot, combine all the ingredients for the Teriyaki sauce.

2. Add the steak and garlic, cover with lid and set the valve to "seal".

3. Choose "Meat/Stew" and adjust to 40 minutes cooking time at high pressure. At the end of the cooking time, allow the pressure to release naturally.

Honey Balsamic Beef (Paleo, AIP)

Tender and juicy beef with delicious honey balsamic broth.

Preparation time: 20 minutes

Cooking time: 35 minutes

Servings: 6

Ingredients:

3 pounds boneless chuck steak

1 teaspoon ground ginger

1 1/2 teaspoons salt

2 tablespoon olive oil

1 teaspoon finely chopped garlic

1/2 cup balsamic vinegar

1 1/2 cup bone broth

3 tablespoons honey

Directions:

1. Trim all visible fat from the steak and slice into 1/2-inch strips.

2. In a small bowl, mix together ground ginger and salt. Rub the mixture all over the meat.

3. Select the "sauté" function on your Instant Pot and add oil. When the oil is hot, brown the beef on all sides, working in batches. Transfer browned beef to a plate and set aside.

4. Select the "sauté" function again then add the garlic and cook for about 1 minute.

5. Stir in broth, balsamic vinegar and honey. Return the browned beef and any accumulated juices to the pot.

6. Cover with lid and set the valve to "seal". Choose "Meat/Stew" and adjust to 35 minutes cooking time at high pressure. At the end of the cooking time, use the quick release method to release the pressure.

7. If you want a thicker sauce, mix 2-3 tablespoons of arrowroot powder with a little water and stir into the pot. Then cook for 5 more minutes. Serve.

Japanese Cream Stew (Paleo, AIP)

Preparation time: 15 minutes

Cooking time: 30 minutes

Servings: 4-6

Ingredients:

1 pound beef, cubed

6 cups water

2 cups beef bone broth

1 white onion, diced

1 medium-ripe plantain, peeled, cut into 1-inch chunks

2 carrots, chopped into 1-inch chunks

2 white turnips, chopped into 1-inch chunks

2 garlic cloves, peeled, chopped

1 bay leaf

1 teaspoon sea salt, divided

1/2 teaspoon cinnamon

1/2 teaspoon dried basil

1 teaspoon honey

1/4 cup coconut flour

2 cups coconut milk

1 broccoli, cut into florets

Directions:

1. Select the "Sauté" function then adjust to "more" mode. Add the 6 cups of water and bring to boil.

2. Add the meat and let boil for 3 minutes. Remove the meat, strain, discard the water and clean the pot.

3. Return meat to the pot then add broth, white onion, plantain, carrots, turnips, garlic, bay leaf, 1/2 teaspoon sea salt, cinnamon and basil. Stir everything together.

4. Cover with lid and set the valve to "seal". Choose "Manual" and adjust to 15-20 minutes cooking time at high pressure. At the end of the cooking time, use the quick release method to release the pressure.

5. Remove the meat and vegetables and leave the broth in the pot.

6. Select the "Sauté" function then stir in honey, coconut flour and coconut milk. Add the broccoli florets then let simmer until broccoli is cooked and gravy is thickened.

7. Remove bay leaf and discard. Return meat and vegetables to the pot and stir gently with the sauce. Add the remaining salt or more if necessary. Serve immediately.

Braised Lamb Shanks With Figs (Paleo, AIP)

A nutrient dense comfort food that also satisfies your dietary needs.

Preparation time: 20 minutes

Cooking time: 90 minutes

Servings: 4

Ingredients:

4 (12-ounce) lamb shanks

2 tablespoons coconut oil

2 tablespoons minced fresh ginger

1 large onion, sliced thinly

2 teaspoons fish sauce

2 tablespoons apple cider vinegar

2 tablespoons coconut aminos

1 1/2 cups bone broth

2-3 garlic cloves, finely minced

10 dried figs, stems cut off, halved lengthwise

Directions:

1. Preheat the Instant Pot by pressing the "sauté" function then add 1 tablespoon of coconut oil.

2. Working in batches, add the lamb shanks to the pot and brown on all sides. Add the remaining coconut oil for the second batch. Transfer browned meat to a plate.

3. Add the ginger and onion. Cook and stir until tender, about 3 minutes.

4. Stir in the fish sauce, apple cider vinegar, coconut aminos, broth, garlic cloves and figs. Stir and scrape up any browned bits.

5. Returned the browned shanks, along with any accumulated juices to the pot. Push the shanks into the liquid as much as possible.

6. Cover with lid and set the valve to "seal". Choose "Manual" and adjust to 60 minutes cooking time at high pressure. At the end of the cooking time, allow the pressure to release naturally.

7. Open the lid and transfer lamb shanks to a platter. Skim fat off the surface of the sauce then serve sauce over lamb shanks. Serve with cauliflower rice.

Curry Lamb Stew With Rosemary (Paleo, AIP, Gluten-Free)

Preparation time: 20 minutes

Cooking time: 35 minutes

Servings: 4

Ingredients:

2 pounds lamb ribs

1 teaspoon turmeric

1 teaspoon Himalayan pink salt

1 cup chopped celery

1 cup chopped carrots

3 fresh rosemary sprigs

6-8 cups roughly chopped cabbage

For the Sauce:

1 cup bone broth

2 cups cooked butternut squash

1 inch of fresh ginger

2 garlic cloves

4-5 mint leaves

Juice of 1 lime

1 teaspoon turmeric

1/2 teaspoon Himalayan pink salt

Directions:

1. Season lamb all over with turmeric and pink salt.

2. In the Instant Pot, combine the lamb, celery, carrots, rosemary and cabbage.

3. Combine the sauce ingredients in a blender then blend until smooth.

4. Pour the sauce over the lamb and vegetables.

5. Cover with lid and set the valve to "seal". Choose "Meat/Stew" and adjust to 35 minutes cooking time at high pressure. Use the 10-minute Natural Release.

Beef Noodle Soup (Paleo, AIP)

Healthy and deliciously satisfying.

Preparation time: 10 minutes

Cooking time: 50 minutes

Servings: 6-8

Ingredients:

1 1/2 pounds boneless chuck steak

2 carrots, sliced

1 cup sliced mushrooms

3 garlic cloves

1 tablespoon fish sauce

2 tablespoons coconut aminos

Filtered water

1 (8-ounce) bag yam noodles, drained, rinsed

Salt, to taste

1/4 cup of chopped fresh cilantro, garnish

Directions:

1. In the instant pot, combine the meat, carrots, mushrooms, garlic, fish sauce and coconut aminos. Add enough water to cover.

2. Cover with lid and set the valve to "seal". Choose "Soup" and adjust to 40 minutes cooking time at high pressure.

3. At the end of the cooking time, use the 10-minute Natural Release.

4. Open the lid, stir in the yam noodles, season with salt and stir again. Serve, garnished with fresh cilantro.

Braised Mexican Beef (Paleo)

Preparation time: 10 minutes

Cooking time: 35 minutes

Servings: 4-6

Ingredients:

2½ pounds boneless beef brisket or beef chuck roast, cubed

1½ teaspoons kosher salt

1 tablespoon chili powder

1 tablespoon ghee or fat of choice

1 medium onion, sliced thinly

6 garlic cloves, peeled, crushed

1 tablespoon tomato paste

½ cup bone broth

½ teaspoon fish sauce

½ cup roasted tomato salsa

Freshly ground black pepper

2 radishes, thinly sliced (optional)

½ cup minced cilantro (optional)

Directions:

1. In a large bowl, mix together beef, salt and chili powder.

2. Select "Sauté" on the Instant Pot and add the ghee. When the fat has melted, add onions and cook until tender.

71

3. Stir in garlic and tomato paste. Cook for 30 seconds.

4. Add the beef then pour in broth, fish sauce tomato salsa. Press "Keep Warm/Cancel" to stop sautéing.

5. Cover with lid and set the valve to "seal". Choose "Meat/Stew" and adjust to 30 minutes cooking time at high pressure. At the end of the cooking time, allow the pressure to release naturally.

6. Open the lid and season with salt and pepper to taste. Serve beef with the sauce along with radishes and cilantro if you like.

Instant Pot Beef Short Ribs (Paleo)

Preparation time: 10 minutes

Cooking time: 45 minutes

Servings: 4

Ingredients:

2 pounds boneless beef short ribs

1 onion, diced

1 tablespoon Szechuan peppercorns

2 tablespoons curry powder (optional)

2 tablespoons vodka

3 tablespoons of coconut aminos

1 cup water

1 tablespoon salt

Directions:

1. Combine all the ingredients in the Instant Pot.

2. Cover with lid and set the valve to "seal". Choose "Meat/Stew" and adjust to 45 minutes cooking time at high pressure.

3. At the end of the cooking time, use the quick release method to release the pressure.

Instant Pot Corned Beef And Cabbage (Paleo)

Preparation time: 10 minutes

Cooking time: 2 hours

Servings: 6

Ingredients:

1 corned beef brisket (3-4 pounds)

4 cups water

3 garlic cloves, peeled, crushed

1 small onion, peeled, quartered

1 teaspoon dried thyme

1/2 teaspoon whole allspice berries (optional)

3 whole black peppercorns (optional)

2 bay leaves

1 head cabbage, cut into wedges

5 medium carrots, peeled, cut into chunks

1 1/2 pounds small red potatoes

Directions:

1. In the Instant Pot, combine corned beef, water, garlic cloves, onions, thyme, allspice, peppercorns and bay leaves.

2. Cover with lid and set the valve to "seal". Choose "Manual" and adjust to 90 minutes cooking time at high pressure. At the end of the cooking time, use the 10-minute Natural Release.

3. Open the lid, remove and discard bay leaves. Remove the meat, place in a plate and cover loosely with foil.

4. To the liquid in the pot, add cabbage, carrots and potatoes. Cover with lid and set the valve to "seal". Choose "Manual" and adjust to 10 minutes cooking time at high pressure.

5. At the end of the cooking time, use the quick release method to release the pressure.

6. Remove the vegetables using a slotted spoon. Slice the corned beef and serve with vegetables and some of the cooking liquid.

PORK MAIN DISHES

Sweet And Zesty Pulled Pork (Paleo, AIP)

Serve this over a bowl of cauliflower rice and you will have a hearty dinner.

Preparation time: 10 minutes

Cooking time: 85 minutes

Servings: 6

Ingredients:

2 pounds boneless pork roast

1 tablespoon ghee or lard

10 ounces bone broth

12 ounces frozen or fresh cranberries

2 tablespoon apple cider vinegar

2 tablespoon chopped fresh herbs (such as marjoram, sage, oregano)

1 tablespoon honey

¼ teaspoon granulated garlic

1/8 teaspoon ground cloves

¼ teaspoon cinnamon

Sea salt

Directions:

1. Select the "sauté" function on your Instant Pot then add the fat.

2. Rub pork on all sides with salt generously. Add pork to hot oil and brown on each side for about 2 minutes. Leave the pork in the pot.

3. Add the broth, cranberries and apple cider vinegar. Top with the herbs and honey.

4. Close the lid and seal. Select "Manual" on the Instant Pot, then adjust to 70 minutes cooking time at high pressure.

5. Use Quick Release to release the pressure. Transfer pork to a cutting board then shred using two forks.

6. Return the meat to the Instant Pot. Season with a little more salt, choose "Manual" again and cook for 10 minutes at high pressure.

7. Remove cranberries and pork from the pot and place in a serving dish. To the serving dish, add garlic, cloves and cinnamon then toss to combine.

8. Serve warm over cauliflower rice.

Paleo Braised Pork (Paleo, AIP)

A different way to make a classic Chinese dish.

Preparation time: 10 minutes

Cooking time: 20 minutes

Servings: 4-6

Ingredients:

2 pounds pork cheek or belly, cut into small pieces

3 tablespoons coconut aminos

3 tablespoons blackstrap molasses

1 inch ginger, peeled, sliced thickly

6 garlic cloves, smashed

2 strips mace

1/2 teaspoon ground cinnamon

2/3 cup bone broth or water

1 teaspoon sea salt

Directions:

1. Select the "Sauté" function and when hot, add all the ingredients and stir for a while.

2. Cover the Instant Pot lid then seal. Select "Manual" function and adjust to 20 minutes cooking time at high pressure.

3. At the end of the cooking time, release pressure with the quick release method. Carefully remove the cover then transfer the meat to a plate and set aside.

4. Select the "Sauté" function and let the sauce in the pot boil until it is slightly thickened.

5. Serve pork with sauce and garnish with coriander leaves.

Red-Cooked Pork (Paleo, AIP)

A feel-good Asian dish that you will always enjoy cooking.

Preparation time: 5 minutes

Cooking time: 45 minutes

Servings: 4

Ingredients:

2 pounds pork belly, cubed

2 tablespoons maple syrup

3 tablespoons sherry

1 tablespoons blackstrap molasses

2 tablespoons coconut aminos

1 teaspoon sea salt

1/3 cup bone broth or water

1 inch fresh ginger, peeled, smashed

A few sprigs of cilantro or coriander leaves, to garnish

Directions:

1. Add pork cubes to a pot then add enough water to cover the meat. Set on high heat and bring to a boil. Let boil for 3 minutes. Drain the pork, rinse off any scum and set aside in a colander.

2. Select the "sauté" function then add maple syrup to the Instant Pot's inner pot.

3. When the maple syrup is hot, add the pork cubes and brown for about 10 minutes.

4. Stir in the remaining ingredients.

5. Cover with lid and set the valve to "seal". Select "Manual" and adjust to 25 minutes cooking time at high pressure. At the end of the cooking time, allow the pressure to release naturally.

6. Open the lid and select the "Sauté" function. Let the sauce in the pot boil gently until it is slightly thickened.

7. Serve, garnished with cilantro or coriander leaves.

Instant Pot Kalua Pig (Paleo, AIP)
A faster and better way to make this traditional Hawaiian dish.

Preparation time: 15 minutes

Cooking time: 1 hour 45 minutes

Servings: 8

Ingredients:

3 slices of bacon

5 pounds of bone-in pork shoulder roast

6 garlic cloves, peeled

Kosher salt, to taste

1 cup water

1 cabbage, cored, cut into 6 wedges

Directions:

1. Add the pieces of bacon to the Instant Pot. Select the "Sauté" function and start frying the bacon. When one side is browned, flip and brown the other side, then turn off the heat.

2. Meanwhile, slice the pork roast into 3 pieces. Cut 2 slits in each piece of pork roast and tuck in the garlic cloves. Season the pork evenly with kosher salt

3. Arrange the pork on the bacon in a single layer then add 1 cup of water.

4. Cover with lid and set the valve to "seal". Choose "Manual" and adjust to 90 minutes cooking time at high pressure. At the end of the cooking time, use the 10-minute Natural Release.

5. By now, the pork should be fork-tender. If it is not, cook under pressure for 10 minutes more. Transfer the pork to a large bowl.

6. Taste the cooking liquid and add more seasoning if necessary.

7. Add the cabbage wedges to the cooking liquid. Cover with lid and seal. Choose "Manual" and adjust to 4-5 minutes cooking time at high pressure. Release the pressure using the quick release method.

8. Meanwhile, use two forks to shred the pork. Serve pork, topped with cabbage and sauce.

Pineapple Pork Stew (Paleo, AIP)
A sweet combination of pork and pineapples with warming spices.

Preparation time: 15 minutes, plus 1 hour marinating

Cooking time: 50 minutes

Servings: 6

Ingredients:

2 tablespoons bacon fat

2 pounds stewing pork, cubed

1 tablespoon coconut aminos

1/2 teaspoon turmeric powder

1/2 teaspoon ginger powder

1/2 teaspoon ground cloves

1/2 teaspoon sea salt

1 large onion, sliced

2 large garlic cloves, chopped

1 cup bone broth

1 cup bite-sized pineapple chunks

1 teaspoon ground cinnamon

2 tablespoons sugar-free marmalade

1 bay leaf

1 bunch Swiss chard, (separate leaves from stems, chop stems finely and cut leaves into inch thick strips)

Directions:

1. Combine coconut aminos, turmeric powder, ginger powder, ground cloves and sea salt in a bowl. Add the pork and allow to marinate for about 1 hour.

2. Select "Sauté" function and add bacon fat to the Instant Pot. Add onions and cook for 1-2 minutes. Add the garlic and cook until garlic is fragrant and onions are translucent. Remove garlic and onions and set aside.

3. If necessary, add more oil to the pot. Working in batches, brown the marinated pork in hot oil. Remove browned pork and set aside.

4. Add broth to the pot and scrape off any browned bits. Return the pork, garlic and onions to the pot. Stir in pineapple chunks, cinnamon, marmalade, bay leaf and chopped Swiss chard stems.

5. Cover with lid and set the valve to "seal". Choose "Meat/Stew" and adjust to 30 minutes cooking time at high pressure. At the end of the cooking time, quick release the pressure.

6. Select the "Sauté" function and gently stir in the Swiss chard leaves. Let simmer until the sauce is slightly thickened and the Swiss chard leaves are cooked.

7. Remove the bay leaf and discard. Adjust seasoning to taste and serve.

Instant Pot Pork Carnitas (Paleo, AIP)

Preparation time: 10 minutes

Cooking time: 45 minutes

Servings: 6

Ingredients:

3 pound boneless pork shoulder, cut into 4 equal pieces

1 teaspoon garlic powder

1 teaspoon onion powder

2 teaspoons dried oregano

2 teaspoons kosher salt

1 tablespoon coconut oil or avocado oil

1 tablespoon minced fresh ginger

4 garlic cloves, chopped

1 medium onion, sliced

1 1/2 cups broth

Chopped cilantro and fresh limes, for serving

Directions:

1. In a small bowl, mix together garlic powder, onion powder, oregano and salt. Rub on all sides of the pork. You can do this a few hours before you cook.

2. Select the "sauté" function on the Instant Pot. When hot, add the oil then brown the pork pieces on all sides.

3. Add the ginger, garlic, onion and broth.

4. Cover with lid and set the valve to "seal". Choose "Meat/Stew" and adjust to 35 minutes cooking time at high pressure. At the end of the cooking time, allow the pressure to release naturally.

5. Remove the meat and pull apart with two forks then return meat to the pot.

6. Serve immediately with cilantro and fresh limes.

Minced Pork With Cabbage (Paleo, AIP)

Hot wholesome food that is quick, easy and full of natural sweetness.

Preparation time: 10 minutes

Cooking time: 10 minutes

Servings: 4-6

Ingredients:

1 tablespoon bacon fat/coconut oil

1 shallot, chopped

1 pound lean minced pork

½ head medium red cabbage, cut into bite-sized pieces

½ head medium green cabbage, cut into bite-sized pieces

1 carrot, peeled, sliced

¼ preserved lemon, diced (optional)

3 garlic cloves, chopped

½ cup bone broth

Coconut aminos, to taste

Sea salt, to taste

1 sheet toasted seaweed

Directions:

1. Preheat the Instant Pot with the 'sauté' setting. When hot, add the oil/fat, then add shallots. Cook until light brown.

2. Working in batches, brown the minced pork in the pot. When you are done, press "Keep warm/cancel".

3. Add the remaining ingredients except coconut aminos and sea salt.

4. Cover with lid and set the valve to "seal". Choose "Manual" and adjust to 3 minutes cooking time at high pressure.

5. At the end of the cooking time, quick release the pressure.

6. Stir in the coconut aminos and salt. Serve hot.

Pork Soup With Watercress And Pear (Paleo, AIP)

The delicate taste of watercress in this soup is a pleasant surprise.

Preparation time: 20 minutes

Cooking time: 40 minutes

Servings: 4-6

Ingredients:

2 pounds pork ribs, cut into individual ribs

Water for blanching pork ribs

1 heaped tablespoon dried figs, rinsed

1 Asian pear, peeled, cored, cut into wedges

1 heaped tablespoon conpoy (dried scallops), soaked in hot water for 15 minutes

1 heaped tablespoon dried red dates/jujubes, pitted, rinsed

8 cups water

4 cups of watercress (1 bunch)

Sea salt, to taste

Directions:

1. Add pork ribs to the inner pot and cover with water. Press the "Sauté" function and let boil for 3 minutes. Remove the ribs, strain, discard the water and clean the pot.

2. Return the meat to the pot with all ingredients except sea salt and watercress.

3. Cover with lid and set the valve to "seal". Choose "Soup" and adjust to 30 minutes cooking time at high pressure.

4. At the end of the cooking time, use the 10-minute Natural Release.

5. Remove lid and use a ladle to skim off oil and scum.

6. Select "Sauté", bring to a boil then stir in the watercress.

7. Press "keep warm/cancel", cover with lid and seal. Select "Soup" and adjust to 3 minutes cooking time at high pressure.

8. At the end of the cooking time, use the 10-minute Natural Release.

9. Season with sea salt and serve immediately.

Pork Belly And Spicy Cauliflower Rice (Paleo, AIP)
An easy one pot dish packed with nourishing flavor.

Preparation time: 15 minutes

Cooking time: 15 minutes

Servings: 4

Ingredients:

4 cups "riced" cauliflower

1 pound pork belly, cooked, cubed

1/2 red onion, sliced

2 green onions, sliced

3 garlic cloves, sliced

1/2 cup bone broth

1/2 cup cilantro, divided

1 tablespoon lime juice

1 tablespoon animal fat (bacon, lard etc.)

1 tablespoon oregano

1 teaspoon turmeric

1/2 teaspoon salt

Directions:

1. Combine all the ingredients in the Instant Pot.

2. Cover with lid and set the valve to "seal". Choose "Manual" and adjust to 15 minutes cooking time at high pressure.

3. At the end of the cooking time, use the 10-minute Natural Release.

Sweet And Sour Spareribs (Clean eating)

Preparation time: 10 minutes

Cooking time: 15 minutes

Servings: 4-6

Ingredients:

4 pounds of ribs, fat trimmed and cut into serving sizes

1 tablespoon canola oil, or preferred frying oil

1 medium onion sliced

1/4 cup ketchup

1/4 reduced-sodium soy sauce

1/3 cup brown sugar

1/3 cup apple cider vinegar

1 (20-ounce) can of pineapple

2 garlic cloves, chopped

1 teaspoon, finely chopped ginger

1 teaspoon fish sauce

1 teaspoon chili powder

1 teaspoon ground coriander

1 pinch smoked paprika

Salt and pepper to taste

Corn starch slurry

Directions:

1. Heat oil in the Instant Pot, using the "sauté" function. Add the onion and cook until translucent.

2. Add the other ingredients except the cornstarch slurry. Press the spareribs into the sauce to submerge. If you are not in a hurry, place the pot in the refrigerator to marinate for a few hours.

3. Cover with lid and set the valve to "seal". Choose "Meat/Stew" and adjust to 12 minutes cooking time at high pressure. At the end of the cooking time, use the 10-minute Natural Release.

4. Open the lid carefully and transfer the meat to a plate.

5. Press "sauté" and bring the sauce to a boil. Stir in the cornstarch slurry until it thickens to your desire.

6. Serve with rice and vegetables.

Ham, Beans And Greens (Clean eating)

Just throw these together and you will be surprised at the outcome.

Preparation time: 5 minutes

Cooking time: 25 minutes

Servings: 8

Ingredients:

1 pound dried great northern beans, sorted, washed

8 cups water

1 pound ham, cut into bite size pieces

1/2 teaspoon garlic powder

2 teaspoons onion powder

Fresh ground black pepper, to taste

2 dried bay leaves

1 (10-ounce) package of frozen chopped spinach

1 dash nutmeg

Directions:

1. Combine beans and water in the Instant Pot.

2. Add the ham, garlic powder, onion powder, pepper and bay leaves.

3. Cover with lid and set the valve to "seal". Choose "Manual" and adjust to 25 minutes cooking time at high pressure.

4. At the end of the cooking time, use the quick release method to release the pressure.

5. Open the lid and stir in the spinach and nutmeg. Press "sauté" and let simmer for a couple of minutes.

6. Serve with crusty bread.

One Pot Pork Loin Dinner (Clean eating, Gluten free)

Preparation time: 25 minutes

Cooking time: 29 minutes

Servings: 4

Ingredients:

1 tablespoon olive oil

1 pound boneless pork loin, cubed

1 small onion, peeled, diced

Salt, to taste

Freshly ground black pepper, to taste

1 cup chicken broth

1/2 cup white wine

1 large turnip, peeled, diced

1 rutabaga, peeled, diced

4 small red potatoes, scrubbed, quartered

1/2 cup sliced leeks, white part only

1 stalk celery, diced finely

4 carrots, peeled, diced

2 teaspoons dried parsley

1/4 teaspoon dried thyme

1/2 teaspoon mild curry powder

3 tablespoons fresh lemon juice

2 Granny Smith apples, peeled, cored, diced

Directions:

1. Press "sauté" and heat oil in the Instant Pot. Add the onion and sauté for 3 minutes.

2. Add the pork, season lightly with salt and pepper then stir-fry until just brown, about 5 minutes.

3. Add the chicken broth, white wine, turnip, rutabaga, potatoes, leeks, celery and carrots. Stir in the parsley, thyme, curry powder and lemon juice.

4. Cover with lid and set the valve to "seal". Choose "Manual" and adjust to 15 minutes cooking time at high pressure. At the end of the cooking time, allow the pressure to release naturally.

5. Open the lid carefully, add the diced apples then press "sauté" and let simmer for 5-6 minutes.

SEAFOOD AND FISH MAIN DISHES

Seafood Chowder (Clean eating, Gluten free)
This chowder is great with dinner rolls and tossed salad.

Preparation time: 25 minutes

Cooking time: 12 minutes

Servings: 6

Ingredients:

2 tablespoons butter

2 large leeks, root ends cut off, bruised outer leaves discarded

2 cups water

4 cups clam juice of fish broth

6 medium russet potatoes, peeled, diced

1 bay leaf

Salt, to taste

Freshly ground black pepper, to taste

1 pound firm white fish (such as scrod), cut into bite size pieces

1/2 cup fat free half-and-half

1/2 teaspoon dried thyme

Directions:

1. Melt butter in the Instant Pot, using the "sauté" function.

2. Slice the leeks and add to the Instant Pot. Sauté for 2 minutes.

3. Stir in water, clam juice or fish broth, potatoes, bay leaf, salt and pepper.

4. Cover with lid and set the valve to "seal". Choose "Manual" and adjust to 4 minutes cooking time at high pressure. At the end of the cooking time, use the quick release method to release the pressure.

5. Open the lid, remove bay leaf and discard.

6. Add the fish, press "sauté" and let simmer for 3 minutes.

7. Stir in half-and-half and thyme. Let heat through with occasional stirring.

Steamed White Fish (Paleo, Gluten free)

This flavorful and healthy dish is ready in less than 15 minutes.

Preparation time: 10 minutes

Cooking time: 5 minutes

Servings: 4

Ingredients:

4 white fish fillets (Haddock etc)

1 cup olives

1 pound cherry tomatoes, sliced

1 large pinch of fresh thyme

1 garlic clove, crushed

Olive oil

Salt and pepper, to taste

Directions:

1. Press "sauté" and add 1 cup of water to the Instant Pot.

2. Arrange the fish fillets in a single layer in the steaming basket. Add sliced olives and cherry tomatoes on top of the fillets. Next, layer some fresh thyme, crushed garlic, olive oil, and salt.

3. Place the steaming basket inside the Instant Pot.

4. Cover with lid and set the valve to "seal". Choose "Manual" and adjust to 3-5 minutes cooking time at high pressure. At the end of the cooking time, use the 10-minute Natural Release.

5. Serve fillets in separate plates, sprinkle with pepper, more thyme and drizzle with olive oil.

Mediterranean Steamed Fish (Paleo, Gluten free)

Here is another way to make steamed fish with a surprisingly pleasing result.

Preparation time: 5 minutes

Cooking time: 8 minutes

Servings: 4

Ingredients:

4 white fish fillets (cod etc)

1 pound cherry tomatoes, sliced

1 bunch of fresh thyme, a few sprigs reserved

1 garlic clove, crushed

Olive oil

2 tablespoon pickled capers

1 cup olives

Salt and pepper, to taste

Directions:

1. In a heatproof bowl (that can fit in the Instant Pot), layer cherry tomatoes and fresh thyme. Next layer fish then add crushed garlic, salt and olive oil.

2. Place the bowl in the Instant Pot.

3. Cover with lid and set the valve to "seal". Choose "Manual" and adjust to 8 minutes cooking time at Low pressure. At the end of the cooking time, use the 10-minute Natural Release.

4. Serve fillets in separate plates, sprinkle with pepper, more thyme, olives, capers and drizzle with olive oil.

Shrimp And Spinach Risotto (Clean eating, Gluten free)

Fast one-dish seafood meal for easy dinners.

Preparation time: 10 minutes

Cooking time: 12 minutes

Servings: 4

Ingredients:

1 tablespoon olive oil

1 tablespoon unsalted butter

1 medium onion, coarsely chopped

1 garlic clove, crushed

1 stick celery, coarsely chopped

1 cup Arborio rice

1/4 teaspoon ground white pepper

2 teaspoon ground oregano

1/4 cup dry white wine

2 1/4 cup low salt chicken broth

2 bay leaves

2 cups fresh spinach, chopped

14-16 medium shrimp (frozen or fresh, uncooked, peeled)

1/2 cup parmesan cheese, finely grated

Directions:

1. If the shrimp is frozen, place them in cold water to thaw while cooking the rice.

2. Press "sauté" on the Instant Pot then add butter and oil. When butter is melted, add onions, garlic and celery. Sauté until onions are soft, or about 2-3 minutes

3. Add rice and stir to coat. Sauté for about 1 minute then add white pepper, oregano, wine, chicken broth and bay leaves. Stir and bring to a simmer.

4. Cover with lid and set the valve to "seal". Choose "Manual" and adjust to 7 minutes cooking time at high pressure.

5. Meanwhile, chop the spinach and peel the shrimp.

6. At the end of the cooking time, use the quick release method to release the pressure. Open the lid carefully, remove bay leaves and discard.

7. Immediately stir in the spinach and shrimp. Cover and let the hot liquid wilt the spinach and cook the shrimp, about 2 minutes. If you use larger shrimp, you may have to remove the lid and press "sauté" to add enough heat. Shrimp is done when it has fully turned pink.

8. Stir in the grated parmesan before serving.

Peruvian Seafood Stew (Clean eating, Gluten free)

A South American one-pot seafood dish.

Preparation time: 20 minutes

Cooking time: 15 minutes

Servings: 5-6

Ingredients:

1 1/2 tablespoons olive oil

2 teaspoons whole cumin seeds

1 large onion, coarsely chopped

1/2 teaspoon sweet paprika

1/4 teaspoon crushed red pepper flakes

3 cups fish broth

1 1/4 pounds Yukon Gold potatoes, peeled, cut into 1/2-inch pieces

2 large bay leaves

1 1/2 pounds of butternut squash, peeled, cut into 1 1/2-inch chunks

1 (15-ounce) can diced tomatoes, with liquid

1 teaspoon salt, or to taste

1 teaspoon dried oregano leaves

2 garlic cloves, crushed

1 pound white fish fillets, (monkfish, haddock or white snapper), cut into bite-size pieces

1/2 pound of medium shrimp, shelled, deveined

2 tablespoons of freshly squeezed lime juice

1/4 cup of chopped fresh cilantro

Directions:

1. Press "sauté" and heat oil the Instant Pot. Add cumin and onions. Cook and stir for 2 minutes.

2. Add sweet paprika, red pepper flakes, fish broth, potatoes and bay leaves. Place the butternut squash chunks on top. Pour tomatoes over butternut squash chunks and sprinkle with some salt. Do not stir.

3. Cover with lid and set the valve to "seal". Choose "Manual" and adjust to 3 minutes cooking time at high pressure. Quick release the pressure and carefully remove the lid.

4. Stir in oregano and garlic. Remove and discard bay leaves.

5. Set the Instant Pot on "sauté" again and bring to a boil. Add the fish and cook for about 2 minutes, uncovered. Add the shrimp and cook for additional 1-2 minutes, or until shrimp turns pink and the fish is opaque and flakes easily with a fork.

6. Taste and add more salt if necessary. Stir in lime juice and cilantro. Serve immediately.

Instant Pot Shrimp Scampi Paella (Clean eating, Gluten free)

Preparation time: 10 minutes

Cooking time: 5 minutes

Servings: 4

Ingredients:

1 pound frozen shrimp (shell on)

1 cup jasmine rice

1/4 cup of butter

1 teaspoon sea salt

1/4 teaspoon of black pepper

1/4 cup chopped fresh parsley

1 pinch crushed red pepper

1 pinch saffron

1 lemon, juiced

4 garlic cloves, minced

1 1/2 cups chicken broth or water

Optional Garnishes:

Chopped fresh parsley

Grated parmesan or Romano cheese

Butter

Fresh Lemon Juice

Directions:

1. In the Instant Pot, combine all the ingredients, placing the shrimp on top.

2. Cover with lid and set the valve to "seal". Choose "Manual" and adjust to 5 minutes cooking time at high pressure. At the end of the cooking time, use the quick release method to release the pressure.

3. Remove the cooked shrimp gently and peel the shell and discard. Return shrimp to the pot.

4. Serve, garnished with fresh parsley, grated cheese, butter and drizzled with lemon juice.

Spicy Fish Coconut Curry (Paleo, Gluten free)
This dish combines curry, fish and coconut to create a classic flavor that is perfect for lunch or dinner.

Preparation time: 5 minutes

Cooking time: 13 minutes

Servings: 4-6

Ingredients:

Olive oil

6 curry leaves

2 medium onions, sliced

1 tablespoon freshly grated ginger

2 garlic cloves, squeezed

3 tablespoons of Curry Powder mix

2 cups un-sweetened coconut milk

1 1/2 pounds fish fillets, cut into bite-size pieces

1 tomato, chopped

2 green chilies, sliced

Salt, to taste

Juice from 1/2 lemon

Directions:

1. Press "sauté" and heat a little oil in the Instant Pot. Add the curry leaves and fry until golden on the edges, about 1 minute.

2. Add onion, ginger and garlic. Sauté until onion is tender. Add the Curry Powder mix and cook for 2 minutes more.

3. Add coconut milk, stir to deglaze and scrape up browned bits from the bottom of the pot.

4. Add the fish, tomato and green chilies. Stir to coat the fish with the sauce.

5. Cover with lid and set the valve to "seal". Choose "Manual" and adjust to 2-3 minutes cooking time at high pressure. At the end of the cooking time, use the 10-minute Natural Release.

6. Taste and add salt as necessary, drizzle with lemon juice then serve. You can serve alone as a light meal or with cooked rice as a full meal.

Steamed Salmon With Lemon And Herbs (Clean eating, Gluten free)

This recipe has minimal preparation and you still get a lot of flavor.

Preparation time: 10 minutes

Cooking time: 6 minutes

Servings: 4

Ingredients:

3 tablespoons butter

1 1/2 pounds salmon fillets

1 tablespoon minced garlic

2 tablespoons dry white wine

1 cup chicken broth

Juice of 1 lemon

1 tablespoon chopped fresh tarragon

1 tablespoon chopped fresh parsley

1 tablespoon light brown sugar

1/4 teaspoon salt

1/8 teaspoon pepper

Directions:

1. Combine all the ingredients in the Instant Pot.

2. Cover with lid and set the valve to "seal". Choose "Manual" and adjust to 6 minutes cooking time at high pressure.

3. At the end of the cooking time, use the quick release method to release the pressure.

4. Serve with pan juices.

Shrimp And Pasta In Creamy Sauce (Clean eating)

Preparation time: 10 minutes

Cooking time: 10 minutes

Servings: 4

Ingredients:

1 tablespoon olive oil

2/3 cup diced onion

8 ounces of farfalle pasta

12 ounces of frozen shrimp

1 teaspoon Old Bay Seasoning

1 tablespoon minced garlic

2 1/2 cups chicken broth

2 teaspoons all-purpose flour

1 cup grated Parmesan cheese

1/2 cup low-fat milk

Salt and pepper, to taste

Chopped parsley

Directions:

1. Press "sauté" and heat oil in the Instant Pot. Cook onion for about 3 minutes, or until translucent.

2. Add the pasta, shrimp, Old Bay Seasoning and garlic. Pour in the broth.

3. Cover with lid and set the valve to "seal". Choose "Manual" and adjust to 7 minutes cooking time at high pressure. At the end of the cooking time, use the quick release method to release the pressure.

4. Open the lid, press "sauté" and stir in the flour, cheese and milk. Season with salt and pepper. let simmer for about 2 minutes.

5. Sprinkle with chopped parsley then serve.

RICE AND PASTA RECIPES

Instant Pot Macaroni And Cheese (Clean eating)

Preparation time: 5 minutes

Cooking time: 20 minutes

Servings: 6-8

Ingredients:

1 pound dried elbow macaroni (whole wheat)

4 cups water

2 tablespoons butter

1 teaspoon hot pepper sauce

1 tablespoon yellow mustard

2 teaspoons table salt

6 ounces shredded Parmesan cheese

16 ounces shredded cheddar cheese

1 (12-ounce) can evaporated milk

Directions:

1. In the Instant Pot, combine macaroni, 4 cups water, butter, hot pepper sauce, mustard and salt.

2. Cover with lid and set the valve to "seal". Choose "Manual" and adjust to 4 minutes cooking time at high pressure. At the end of the cooking time, use the quick release method to release the pressure.

3. Open the lid and stir in the evaporated milk. Select "sauté" and let simmer until pasta is al dente.

4. Stir in the cheese gradually and keep stirring until melted. Serve.

Instant Pot White Rice (Clean eating, Gluten free)
Your Instant Pot can double perfectly as a rice cooker.

Preparation time: minutes

Cooking time: minutes

Servings: 4-6

Ingredients:

2 cups of long grain white rice

2 1/2 cups of water

1/2 teaspoon of table salt

Directions:

1. Combine rice and water in the Instant Pot. Add salt and stir.

2. Cover with lid and set the valve to "seal". Choose "Manual" and adjust to 4 minutes cooking time at high pressure.

3. At the end of the cooking time, use the 10-minute Natural Release.

4. Use a fork to fluff the rice and serve.

Risotto And Peas (Clean eating, Gluten free)
Get this delicious Mediterranean dish in just a few minutes.

Preparation time: 5 minutes

Cooking time: 17 minutes

Servings: 4

Ingredients:

2 tablespoons canola oil

1 small onion, chopped finely

1 cup Arborio rice

2 1/4 cups chicken stock

1 cup frozen peas

1/8 teaspoon pepper

1/3 cup Parmesan cheese

Directions:

1. Select "sauté" and heat 2 tablespoons of oil in the Instant Pot. Add onion and sauté for about 5 minutes, with frequent stirring.

2. Add rice and cook until light brown. Stir in the chicken stock and peas.

3. Cover with lid and set the valve to "seal". Choose "Manual" and adjust to 8 minutes cooking time at high pressure. At the end of the cooking time, use the quick release method to release the pressure.

4. Stir in pepper and the cheese. Let sit until the cheese melts then stir and serve.

Quick Rice With Vegetables (Clean eating, Gluten free)

Preparation time: 20 minutes

Cooking time: 18 minutes

Servings: 4

Ingredients:

1 cup brown rice

2 cups chicken stock

1 large tomato, peeled, seeded, chopped

1/2 cup of diced celery

1/2 cup of diced carrots

1/2 cup sliced green onion

1/2 cup of diced green pepper

1 (2-ounce) package of sliced blanched almonds

1 1/2 cups of water

1/4 cup of chopped parsley

Directions:

1. In a metal bowl that fits into the Instant Pot, combine rice and chicken stock.

2. Stir in tomato, celery, carrots, green onion, green pepper and almonds.

3. Add 1 1/2 cups of water to the Instant Pot then place the steamer basket inside. Place the metal bowl on the steamer basket.

4. Cover with lid and set the valve to "seal". Choose "Manual" and adjust to 13 minutes cooking time at high pressure. At the end of the cooking time, use the 10-minute Natural Release.

5. Select "sauté" and "Less". Let simmer for 5 minutes then stir in the parsley. Serve with hot sauce at the table.

One Pot Penne Dinner (Clean eating)
Simply throw everything in the pot and dinner is ready!

Preparation time: 10 minutes

Cooking time: 15 minutes

Servings: 10-12

Ingredients:

1 pound penne pasta

1 (24-ounce) jar tomato sauce

2 tablespoons olive oil

1 box beef or chicken broth

1 1/2 pounds ground turkey or beef, crumbled

1/2 cup Parmesan or Romano cheese

1 small onion, diced

1 garlic clove, minced

1/2 teaspoon dried basil

Directions:

1. Combine all the ingredients in your Instant Pot, topping with the meat. Ensure the pot is not more than 2/3 full.

2. Cover with lid and set the valve to "seal". Choose "Manual" and adjust to 15-20 minutes cooking time at high pressure (20 minutes if you use frozen meat).

3. At the end of the cooking time, allow the pressure to release naturally.

4. Stir and serve.

Sausage With Fusilli Pasta (Clean eating)

Serve with garlic bread and tossed salad.

Preparation time: 10 minutes

Cooking time: 20 minutes

Servings: 6

Ingredients:

1 pound of ground sausage

1 tablespoon of olive oil

1 large onion, peeled, diced

3 garlic cloves, peeled, minced

1 cup tomato sauce

3 cups chicken broth

1/2 teaspoon sugar

1 teaspoon dried basil

1/2 teaspoon ground fennel

2 teaspoons dried parsley

1/8 teaspoon dried red pepper flakes

1/4 teaspoon freshly ground black pepper

3 cups Fusilli pasta

1/4 cup half-and-half

Salt, to taste

1/2 cup grated Parmigiano-Reggiano cheese

Directions:

1. Select "sauté" and add sausage to the Instant Pot. Cook sausage, stir and break apart, about 5 minutes. Drain the fat and discard.

2. Add the oil and onion. Cook until onion is tender, about 3 minutes. Stir in the garlic and cook for 30 seconds.

3. Stir in the tomato sauce, broth, sugar, basil, fennel, parsley, red pepper flakes, pepper and pasta.

4. Cover with lid and set the valve to "seal". Choose "Manual" and adjust to 9 minutes cooking time at Low pressure. At the end of the cooking time, use the quick release method to release the pressure.

5. Open the lid and stir in half-and-half. Taste and add salt as necessary.

6. Transfer to a serving platter and serve, topped with cheese.

Linguine With Smoked Trout Sauce (Clean eating)

Preparation time: 7 minutes

Cooking time: 8 minutes

Servings: 6

Ingredients:

1/4 cup olive oil

2 cups linguine

4 cups chicken broth

1 teaspoon dried thyme

1/4 teaspoon freshly ground white pepper

1/2 teaspoon sea salt

3 tablespoons of butter

1/2 cup of light sour cream

1 pound smoked trout, cut in bite-size pieces

2 green onions, cleaned, diced

1/3 cup grated Parmigiano-Reggiano cheese

Directions:

1. Press "sauté" and heat oil in the Instant Pot.

2. Stir in linguine, broth, thyme, pepper and salt.

3. Cover with lid and set the valve to "seal". Choose "Manual" and adjust to 8 minutes cooking time at high pressure. At the end of the cooking time, use the quick release method to release the pressure.

4. Remove the lid and if necessary, drain the pasta then transfer to a serving bowl.

5. Cut butter into small pieces and toss with the pasta. Add the sour cream, smoked trout and green onion. Toss to mix.

6. Top with grated Parmigiano-Reggiano cheese and serve.

10 Minute Saffron Rice (Clean eating, Gluten free)

Preparation time: 5 minutes

Cooking time: 10 minutes

Servings: 8

Ingredients:

2 cups Jasmine Rice

2 tablespoons butter or ghee

1 small onion, chopped finely

3 1/2 cups chicken bone-broth

2 pinches saffron, crushed

1 teaspoon sea salt

Directions:

1. Soak the rice in cool water for about 1 hour then rinse in fresh water 3-4 times. Drain well.

2. Press "sauté" and melt butter in the Instant Pot. Sauté onions until soft.

3. Add the rice then cook and stir for 1 minute. Stir in chicken broth, saffron and sea salt.

4. Cover with lid and set the valve to "seal". Choose "Manual" and adjust to 5 minutes cooking time at Low pressure.

5. At the end of the cooking time, use the quick release method to release the pressure. Remove the lid carefully.

Risotto With Butternut Squash (Clean eating, Gluten free)

This combination of risotto with butternut squash soup is a winner for all!

Preparation time: 20 minutes

Cooking time: 18 minutes

Servings: 6–8

Ingredients:

2 cups cubed butternut squash

1 cup water

1 tablespoon butter

1 tablespoon olive oil

1 small red onion, diced

2 cups Arborio rice

1 tablespoon apple cider vinegar

5 cups chicken broth

1/2 teaspoon ground cinnamon

1 tablespoon chopped fresh sage

1/3 cup half-and-half

1 1/2 tablespoons light brown sugar

Salt to taste

Directions:

1. Combine butternut squash cubes and 1 cup of water in the Instant Pot.

2. Cover with lid and set the valve to "seal". Choose "Manual" and adjust to 6 minutes cooking time at high pressure.

3. At the end of the cooking time, use the quick release method to release the pressure. Drain the squash and set aside in a large mixing bowl. Mash the cooked squash with a potato masher.

4. Clean and dry the Instant Pot. Press "sauté" and heat the butter and oil until butter melts. Add onion and cook for about 5 minutes.

5. Stir in the rice and cook for 1 minute. Add the mashed butternut squash, apple cider vinegar, chicken broth, cinnamon and sage.

6. Cover with lid and set the valve to "seal". Choose "Manual" and adjust to 6 minutes cooking time at high pressure. At the end of the cooking time, use the quick release method to release the pressure.

7. Stir in the half-and-half, season with salt to taste then serve.

VEGETABLE MAIN DISHES

Savoy Cabbage And Creamy Sauce (Paleo, AIP, Gluten free)

Your family will enjoy this dish, and you will have to make it often.

Preparation time: 10 minutes

Cooking time: 9 minutes

Servings: 4-6

Ingredients:

1 cup bacon, diced

1 onion, chopped

2 cups of bone broth

1 medium head Savoy cabbage, finely chopped

1 bay leaf

1/2 can coconut milk (about 1 cup)

1/4 teaspoon mace

Sea salt, to taste

2 tablespoons of parsley flakes

Directions:

1. Cut a parchment round about the size of the bottom of the inner pot. Press "Sauté" to preheat the inner pot.

2. Once the pot is hot, add bacon and onions and cook until onions are translucent and bacon is crisp.

3. Stir in the broth, scraping up browned bits from the bottom of the pot. Stir in cabbage and add the bay leaf.

4. Place the parchment round on top, shut the lid and seal.

5. Choose 'Manual' then adjust to 4 minutes cooking time at high pressure.

6. When you hear the beep at the end of 4 minutes, press "Keep warm/cancel" then use quick release. Open the lid carefully and remove the parchment paper.

7. Press "Sauté" and bring to a boil. Stir in the coconut milk and mace. Let simmer for about 5 minutes and then turn off your Instant Pot.

8. Stir in parsley flakes and serve.

Butternut Squash Soup (Paleo, Gluten free)

Simply toss the ingredients into the Instant Pot, and without further ado, you have a delicious soup with intense flavors.

Preparation time: 20 minutes

Cooking time: 30 minutes

Servings: Yields 4 quarts

Ingredients:

1 butternut squash, peeled, seeded, diced

3 large carrots, diced

1 onion, diced

4 garlic cloves, peeled

2 cups diced celery

1/4 cup parsley leaves

2 tablespoons fresh thyme leaves

6 cups chicken stock

1 1/2 tablespoons salt, plus more to taste

1/4 tablespoons pepper, plus more to taste

1 1/2 cup full fat coconut milk

2 tablespoons dried oregano

1 teaspoon cayenne

3 tablespoons herbs de Provence

Fresh chives (optional)

Directions:

121

1. In the Instant Pot, combine butternut squash, onion, garlic, celery, parsley and thyme.

2. Cover everything with chicken stock then season with salt and pepper.

3. Cover with lid and set the valve to "seal". Choose "Soup" and adjust to 30 minutes cooking time at high pressure.

4. At the end of the cooking time, use quick release to release the pressure.

5. Transfer the soup to a regular blender or use an immersion blender to blend until smooth.

6. Stir in the coconut milk, oregano, cayenne and herbs de Provence. Taste for seasoning and adjust as necessary.

7. If you like, garnish with fresh chives then serve.

Fast And Easy Onion Soup (Clean eating)

This French onion soup will give you the needed comfort on a chilly day.

Preparation time: 5 minutes

Cooking time: 22 minutes

Servings: 4

Ingredients:

2 tablespoons coconut oil or avocado oil

8 cups yellow onions, peel, sliced

6 cups pork stock

1 tablespoon balsamic vinegar

2 bay leaves

1 teaspoon salt

2 large sprigs of fresh thyme

1 baguette, sliced

1 1/2 cups of grated Gruyere cheese

Directions:

1. Add the oil to the Instant Pot and select "Sauté".

2. Add the onions and cook in hot oil, with occasional stirring for about 7 minutes, or until translucent.

3. Add some of the stock and scrape up any browned bits from the bottom of the Instant Pot, then add the remaining stock, balsamic vinegar, bay leaves, salt and thyme.

4. Turn of the Instant Pot then close the lid, and seal. Set to "High Pressure" and cook for 10 minutes.

5. Release the pressure using the natural release. Open the lid and discard the thyme stems and bay leaves.

6. Transfer to a regular blender or use an immersion blender to blend until smooth.

7. Preheat the broiler. Place baguette slices in a single layer on a sheet pan. Sprinkle with cheese and broil until golden brown and bubbly, about 3 to 5 minutes.

8. Serve soup with cheesy bread.

Smothered Greens (Paleo, Gluten free)

This nutritious, colorful and quick dish can be served as a main dish or as a side dish.

Preparation time: 15 minutes

Cooking time: 20 minutes

Servings: 4

Ingredients:

1 tablespoon bacon fat or lard

6 cups of raw greens (mustard, collard, turnip, kale, spinach, etc.)

1 pound fully cooked, uncured ham, cut into chunks

1 onion, chopped

1 turnip, chopped

1/2 cup chicken bone broth

2 garlic cloves, crushed

1/8 teaspoon salt

Directions:

1. Combine all the ingredients in the Instant Pot.

2. Cover with lid and set the valve to "seal". Choose "Manual" and adjust to 20 minutes cooking time at high pressure.

3. At the end of the cooking time, use the 10-minute Natural Release.

4. Open the lid, stir then serve.

Lentil Dal With Spinach (Vegan, Gluten Free)

Delicious peasant food with stewed lentils and spinach.

Preparation time: 10 minutes

Cooking time: 20 minutes

Servings: 6

Ingredients:

2 tablespoons olive or coconut oil

1 large red or yellow onion, chopped

3 garlic cloves, minced

1/4 teaspoon dried cayenne pepper

1 teaspoon ground turmeric

1 teaspoon ground coriander

1 teaspoon ground cumin

3 cups water

1 1/5 cups of red lentils

1 large tomato, cut into wedges

1/2 teaspoon salt

4 cups of spinach

To serve:

Cooked brown rice

Fresh cilantro

Vegan yogurt

Directions:

1. Press the "sauté" function and add oil to the Instant Pot. Add the onions; cook until tender and translucent.

2. Stir in the garlic and cook for 1 minute more.

3. Press the "Cancel" button then add cayenne, turmeric, coriander and cumin. Stir to combine.

4. Add water, lentils, tomato wedges and salt. Stir to mix well.

5. Cover with lid and set the valve to "seal". Choose "Manual" and adjust to 10 minutes cooking time at high pressure. At the end of the cooking time, use the 10-minute Natural Release.

6. Remove tomatoes and discard the skins. Return tomatoes to pot then stir, mashing the lentils and smashing tomatoes as you mix.

7. Stir in the spinach and let sit for a couple of minutes.

8. Serve over brown rice and top with vegan yogurt and fresh cilantro.

Mashed Potatoes With Goat Cheese (Clean Eating)
The goat cheese flavor is what makes this dish rich and splendid in taste.

Preparation time: 5 minutes

Cooking time: 40 minutes

Servings: 8-10

Ingredients:

3 pounds Yukon gold potatoes, scrubbed

1 tablespoon kosher salt

1/2 cup fat-free sour cream

1/2 cup milk

8 ounces goat cheese with herbs

2 tablespoons butter

Salt and pepper to taste

Directions:

1. Add the whole potatoes to the Instant Pot then add 1 tablespoon of salt and enough water to cover to about halfway.

2. Cover with lid and set the valve to "seal". Choose "Manual" and adjust to 20 minutes cooking time at high pressure. At the end of the cooking time, allow the pressure to release naturally.

3. Open the lid, drain the potatoes and return them to the pot. If you like, slip off the potato skins.

4. Add sour cream, milk, 3/4 of the goat cheese and butter. Mash well until smooth, using a potato masher.

5. Scoop the mashed potatoes unto an 8-inch baking dish. Add the remaining goat cheese on top and spread with a spoon.

6. Cook under the broiler until golden brown, about 5 minutes.

Mediterranean Vegetable Soup (Clean Eating)

A nourishing pot of cheesy vegetable flavors with fresh herb toppings.

Preparation time: 20 minutes

Cooking time: 35 minutes

Servings: 4

Ingredients:

3 tablespoons olive oil

1 onion, chopped

3 cups shredded cabbage

1 garlic clove, minced

2 celery stalks, chopped

2 medium carrots, chopped

1 (15-ounce) can chickpeas

1 (15-ounce) can fire-roasted diced tomatoes

4 cups vegetable broth or chicken broth

Salt and pepper to taste

To Serve:

1/4 cup crumbled feta cheese

2 tablespoons fresh parsley, chopped

Directions:

1. Set the Instant Pot to "sauté" and add the olive oil. When hot, add the onions and cook with frequent stirring until tender, about 5 minutes.

2. Add cabbage and garlic and cook for 5 minutes more. Stir in the celery, carrots and chickpeas. Again, cook for about 5 minutes.

3. Add the canned tomatoes and broth, then season with salt and pepper. Cancel the "sauté" function.

4. Cover with lid and set the valve to "seal". Choose "Soup" and adjust to 10 minutes cooking time at high pressure. Release pressure using quick release.

5. Open the lid and serve hot. Garnish with parsley and feta cheese

Garlicky Mashed Potatoes (Vegan, Gluten Free)

Preparation time: 10 minutes

Cooking time: 4 minutes

Servings: 4

Ingredients:

4 medium Yukon gold or russet potatoes, cut into chunks

6 garlic cloves, peeled, cut in half

1 cup vegetable broth

1/2 cup non-dairy milk

Salt

Black pepper

1/4 cup chopped parsley

Directions:

1. Add potatoes, garlic and broth to the Instant Pot.

2. Cover with lid and set the valve to "seal". Choose "Manual" and adjust to 4 minutes cooking time at high pressure. At the end of the cooking time, use the 10-minute Natural Release

3. Open the lid and use a masher to mash the potatoes. Add the milk and season with salt and pepper.

4. Stir in the parsley and serve hot.

Risotto With Almond And Coconut (Vegan, Gluten Free)

This Risotto savory and beautiful dish.

Preparation time: 5 minutes

Cooking time: 10 minutes

Servings: 4

Ingredients:

1 cup coconut milk

2 cups vanilla almond milk

1 cup Arborio rice

Dash of cinnamon

2 teaspoons vanilla extract

1/ 3 cup coconut sugar or Sucanat, or more to taste

1/4 cup toasted coconut flakes

Directions:

1. Set the Instant Pot to "sauté" and add the coconut milk and almond milk. Bring to a boil with constant stirring.

2. Stir in the rice and cinnamon then cancel the "sauté" function.

3. Cover with lid and set the valve to "seal". Choose "Manual" and adjust to 5 minutes cooking time at high pressure. At the end of the cooking time, use the 10-minute Natural Release.

4. Stir in the vanilla extract and coconut sugar or Sucanat.

5. Serve the risotto warm, topped with coconut flakes and sliced fruit.

Spicy Pumpkin Soup (Vegan, Gluten Free)

Preparation time: 20 minutes

Cooking time: 10 minutes

Servings: 6

Ingredients:

1 onion, diced

3 garlic cloves, diced

1 teaspoon salt

1 teaspoon black pepper

1/4 teaspoon nutmeg

1 teaspoon cinnamon

1 chipotle pepper in adobe sauce

1 tablespoon adobe sauce (from the chipotle pepper)

1 (15-ounce) can pumpkin puree

2 large green apples, diced

2 cups diced red potatoes

1/4 a cup of almonds (or walnuts), chopped finely

1/4 a cup of uncooked red lentils, chopped finely

2 cups water

2 cups vegetable broth

Directions:

1. Set the Instant Pot to "sauté" and add a little oil. Add onion and garlic then sauté until light brown, about 4 minutes.

2. Stir in the salt, black pepper, nutmeg, cinnamon, chipotle pepper and adobe sauce.

3. Add the pumpkin puree, apples, potatoes, chopped almonds, chopped lentils, water and broth.

4. Cover with lid and set the valve to "seal". Choose "Manual" and adjust to 4 minutes cooking time at high pressure. At the end of the cooking time, use the 10-minute Natural Release.

5. Open the lid carefully and transfer the soup to a food processor or blender.

6. Blend until smooth and serve immediately. You can serve with salad or crusty bread.

Instant Pot Black Bean Soup (Vegan, Gluten Free)

Pull dinner together awesomely with this sumptuous soup.

Preparation time: 5 minutes

Cooking time: 10 minutes

Servings: 4

Ingredients:

1 1/2 cups dry black beans, soaked overnight or quick soaked

1 tablespoon oil

1 onion, chopped

3 garlic cloves, minced

1/4 teaspoon chipotle powder

1 tablespoon ground cumin

6 cups vegetable broth

2 teaspoons dried oregano leaves

1 large bay leaf

1 teaspoons salt, or to taste

Sour cream and chopped cilantro, for garnish

Directions:

1. Drain the soaking water from the beans then set beans aside.

2. Set the Instant Pot to "sauté" and add the oil. Sauté onion in hot oil for about 2 minutes.

3. Stir in garlic, chipotle powder and cumin. Add the broth, beans, oregano and bay leaf. Stir to combine.

4. Cover with lid and set the valve to "seal". Choose "Manual" and adjust to 7 minutes cooking time at high pressure. At the end of the cooking time, allow the pressure to release naturally.

5. Carefully open the lid and remove the bay leaf. Use a potato masher to mash the beans then stir in salt to taste.

6. Serve, garnished with sour cream and cilantro.

Quick Lentil Soup (Vegan)

Preparation time: 5 minutes

Cooking time: 15 minutes

Servings: 8

Ingredients:

2 cups brown lentils

1 large yellow onion, peeled, quartered

4 garlic cloves, peeled

5 plum tomatoes, cut in half, seeded

1 large carrot, peeled

1 tablespoon olive oil

2 teaspoons dried tarragon

1 teaspoon paprika

1 teaspoon dried thyme

6 cups vegetable broth or water

2 bay leaves

1 1/2 teaspoons salt, or to taste

Fresh ground black pepper, to taste

Directions:

1. Combine all the ingredients in the Instant Pot.

2. Press "sauté" and bring to a boil. Cancel the "sauté" function.

3. Cover with lid and set the valve to "seal". Choose "Manual" and adjust to 8 minutes cooking time at high pressure. At the end of the cooking time, use quick release.

4. Carefully open the lid then remove and discard the bay leaf.

5. Carefully transfer onion, garlic, tomatoes and carrots to a blender and puree until smooth.

6. Returned the pureed veggies to the pot and stir.

9. Serve the soup with baguettes.

SIDE DISHES

Hearty Sweet Potato Puree (Paleo, AIP)

Preparation time: 5 minutes

Cooking time: 10 minutes

Servings: 6

Ingredients:

2 pounds sweet potatoes, peeled, cubed

1 1/2 cups bone broth (beef or pork)

1/2 teaspoon sea salt

Directions:

1. Combine sweet potatoes and bone broth in the Instant Pot.

2. Cover with lid and set the valve to "seal". Choose "Manual" and adjust to 10 minutes cooking time at high pressure and cook until potatoes break apart easily with a fork. Quick release the pressure.

3. Transfer sweet potatoes plus broth to a high speed blender or food processor. Add salt then blend until you have a silky puree, about 30 seconds.

4. Serve with a meaty main dish.

Maple Glazed Carrots (Paleo)

Tender and tasty, these carrots are made to be enjoyed.

Preparation time: 5 minutes

Cooking time: 6 minutes

Servings: 6

Ingredients:

2 pounds carrots, peeled, sliced thickly diagonally

1/4 cup raisins

1 cup of water

1 tablespoon maple syrup

1 tablespoon butter

Pepper to taste

Directions:

1. In the Instant pot, combine carrots and raisins with 1 cup of water.

2. Cover with lid and set the valve to "seal". Choose "Manual" and adjust to 4 minutes cooking time at Low pressure. At the end of the cooking time, use the quick release method to release the pressure.

3. Remove carrots and strain.

4. Melt maple syrup and butter briefly in the Instant Pot. Stir well then add the strained carrots. Mix gently until coated.

5. Serve, sprinkled with pepper.

Sweet Potatoes With Maple And Pecans (Clean eating)

This fresh sweet potato dish is a great accompaniment to a meaty meal.

Preparation time: 10 minutes

Cooking time: 9 minutes

Servings: 8

Ingredients:

1/2 cup packed brown sugar

1/4 teaspoon salt

1 1-inch piece lemon peel

1 cup water

3 medium sweet potatoes; peeled, cubed

1/4 cup butter

1/4 cup maple syrup

1 cup pecans, chopped coarsely

1 tablespoon cornstarch

Directions:

1. In the Instant pot, combine brown sugar, salt and lemon peel with 1 cup of water. Stir in the sweet potatoes.

2. Cover with lid and set the valve to "seal". Choose "Manual" and adjust to 4 minutes cooking time at high pressure. At the end of the cooking time, use the quick release method to release the pressure.

3. Open the lid then use a slotted spoon to transfer sweet potatoes to a serving platter.

4. Melt butter on medium heat in a small skillet until bubbly. Stir in pecans, syrup and cornstarch. Blend properly.

5. Add the pecan mixture to the liquid in the Instant Pot. Press the "sauté" function and cook until thickened.

6. Spoon over the sweet potatoes.

Carrots With Garlic And Olives (Paleo)
An amazing dish, full of flavors and vitamins.

Preparation time: 10 minutes

Cooking time: 10 minutes

Servings: 8

Ingredients:

1 tablespoon olive oil

20 whole small garlic cloves

1 large onion peeled, chopped coarsely

1 cup vegetable stock

1/4 cup coarsely chopped olives

1/2 teaspoon dried rosemary leaves

1 pound carrots, cut into 1" chunks

1/4 teaspoon sea salt

Directions:

1. Heat oil in the Instant Pot, using the "sauté" function. Add the garlic and onions. Cook and stir for about 2 minutes.

2. Add the vegetable stock, bring to a boil then stir in olives, rosemary, carrots and sea salt.

3. Cover with lid and set the valve to "seal". Choose "Manual" and adjust to 1 minute cooking time at high pressure. At the end of the cooking time, use the quick release method to release the pressure.

4. Use a slotted spoon to remove the solid ingredients and serve on plates. You can also serve in bowls along with the liquid.

Buttered Beets (Paleo, Gluten free)
This goes well with any meaty main dish.

Preparation time: 5 minutes

Cooking time: 28 minutes

Servings: 8

Ingredients:

4 large red or golden beets

1 cup water

Butter, to taste

Salt, to taste

Freshly ground black pepper, to taste

Directions:

1. Scrub beets and trim both ends. Place the beets on the steaming basket in the Instant Pot. Pour in 1 cup of water.

2. Cover with lid and set the valve to "seal". Choose "Manual" and adjust to 28 minutes cooking time at high pressure. At the end of the cooking time, use the quick release method to release the pressure.

3. Place the beets on a cutting board and let cool.

4. When beets are cool, remove the peel with a knife then slice the beets.

5. Return beet slices to the Instant Pot. Press "sauté", add butter and season with salt and pepper.

Wine Braised Sauerkraut (Clean eating)
Sauerkraut braised in white wine is a great side dish to serve with pork main dishes.

Preparation time: 5 minutes

Cooking time: 25 minutes

Servings: 6

Ingredients:

4 pounds sauerkraut

2 ounces bacon, diced

2 tablespoons unsalted butter

1 teaspoon caraway seed

1 small white onion

2 cups dry white wine

Directions:

1. Rinse the sauerkraut properly then soak in water for 2 hours. Change the soaking water 3-4 times periodically.

2. Select the "sauté" function on your Instant Pot then add the butter and bacon.

3. Cook for about 3 minutes then stir in onions and caraway seeds and cook for additional 3 minutes.

4. Stir in sauerkraut, cook for 3 minutes more then add the wine.

5. Cover with lid and set the valve to "seal". Choose "Manual" and adjust to 15 minutes cooking time at high pressure. At the end of the cooking time, allow the pressure to release naturally.

6. Serve immediately.

Green Beans With Tomato Sauce (Clean eating)

Serve this as a side dish or as a sauce with pasta or rice dishes.

Preparation time: 5 minutes

Cooking time: 15 minutes

Servings: 4-6

Ingredients:

1 garlic clove, crushed

1 tablespoon olive oil

2 cups fresh tomatoes, chopped

1 pound green beans (frozen or fresh), ends removed

Salt

1 teaspoon extra virgin olive oil

143

1 sprig basil, leaves removed

Directions:

1. Select "sauté" to preheat your Instant Pot. Add a little olive oil and garlic.

2. Cook until garlic is golden then stir in the tomatoes.

3. Add the green beans to the steamer basket and sprinkle with salt. Fit the steamer basket into the Instant Pot.

4. Cover with lid and set the valve to "seal". Choose "Manual" and adjust to 5 minutes cooking time at high pressure. At the end of the cooking time, use the quick release method to release the pressure.

5. Open the lid carefully and remove the steamer basket. Pour the beans into tomato sauce in the Instant pot base and mix together.

6. Test the green beans for doneness. If it requires more cooking, cook for a few minutes, uncovered using the "sauté" function.

7. Transfer to a serving bowl, sprinkle with basil and stir in a little olive oil. Serve warm.

Garlic Almond Green Beans (Vegan)
Super-fast side dish of busy nights.

Preparation time: 5 minutes

Cooking time: 5 minute

Servings: 4

Ingredients:

1 teaspoon sesame oil

5 garlic cloves, sliced thinly

1/4 cup water

1 pound green beans, cut into 1/2-inch pieces

1/4 teaspoon sea salt

1/4 cup of slivered almonds

Directions:

1. Press "sauté" on your Instant Pot and heat the oil. Add the garlic and cook until soft, about

2 minutes.

2. Add water and the green beans.

3. Cover with lid and set the valve to "seal". Choose "Manual" and adjust to 1 minute cooking time at high pressure. At the end of the cooking time, use the quick release method to release the pressure.

4. Open the lid carefully, stir in salt and the almond slivers. Serve.

Instant Pot Potato Salad (Clean eating)

You don't have to wait for picnics and barbecues to cook this favorite in your Instant Pot.

Preparation time: 10 minutes

Cooking time: 4 minutes

Servings: 8

Ingredients:

1 1/2 cups water

6 medium russet potatoes, peeled, cubed

4 large eggs

1 small onion, finely chopped

2 tablespoons finely chopped fresh parsley

1 tablespoon dill pickle juice

1 cup mayonnaise

1 tablespoon mustard

Salt and pepper to taste

Directions:

1. Add water to the Instant Pot and put in the steamer basket. Add the potatoes and eggs.

2. Cover with lid and set the valve to "seal". Choose "Manual" and adjust to 4 minutes cooking time at high pressure. At the end of the cooking time, use the quick release method to release the pressure.

3. Carefully remove the lid and bring out the steamer basket. Transfer eggs to ice water to cool. Let potatoes cool slightly.

4. Combine the onion, parsley, pickle juice, mayo and mustard in a large serving bowl. Add the potatoes and mix gently.

5. Peel 3 of the cooked eggs then dice them. Stir diced eggs into the potato mixture. Season with salt and pepper then add more mayonnaise if desired.

6. Place in refrigerator for at least 1 hour before you serve. Slice the remaining boiled eggs and use as garnish.

Brussels Sprouts And Herbs (Vegan)

A delicious alternative to roasting Brussels sprouts.

Preparation time: 20 minutes

Cooking time: 8 minutes

Servings: 4

Ingredients:

1 pound Brussels sprouts, washed

1 tablespoon coarsely chopped garlic

1 tablespoon canola oil

1 teaspoon dried thyme leaves

1 teaspoon whole rosemary leaves

1/4 teaspoon sea salt

1 cup water

Directions:

1. Remove and discard the outer leaves of Brussels sprouts then cut in half. Set aside.

2. Using a mortar and pestle, crumble the thyme and rosemary.

3. Press the "sauté" function and heat oil in your Instant Pot. Stir in the garlic then stir in the Brussels sprouts. Cook and stir frequently for 5 minutes. Add 1 or 2 teaspoons of water to prevent the ingredients sticking to the pan.

4. Stir in thyme, rosemary salt and water.

5. Cover with lid and set the valve to "seal". Choose "Manual" and adjust to 1 minute cooking time at high pressure. At the end of the cooking time, use the quick release method to release the pressure.

6. Remove the lid carefully and serve immediately.

DESSERTS

Quick And Easy Applesauce (Paleo, AIP, Gluten free)

Preparation time: 10 minutes

Cooking time: 10 minutes

Servings: Yields 1 quart

Ingredients:

12 medium apples, peeled, cored, diced

½ cup apple juice

Directions:

1. Cut a parchment round about the size of the bottom of the inner pot

2. Combine apples and apple juice in the inner pot of your Instant Pot.

3. Place the parchment round over the apples. Shut the lid and seal.

4. Choose "Manual" then adjust to 10 minutes cooking time at high pressure. At the end of the cooking time, release the pressure naturally.

5. Remove the lid and discard the parchment paper.

6. Transfer to a regular blender or use an immersion blender to blend until smooth.

Honey Cashew Cream With Fruits (Clean eating, Paleo)

Preparation time: 4 minutes

Cooking time: 8 minutes

Servings: 4

Ingredients:

1/4 cup honey

2 cups water

1 cup carrot, sliced

1/2 pound mixed dried fruit

2 teaspoons lemon rind, grated

1/2 cup raisins

1/4 teaspoon ground cinnamon

1 tablespoon of arrowroot

1/2 cup cashews

Directions:

1. Combine honey and water in the Instant Pot. Press "sauté" and bring to a simmer.

2. Add the carrots, dried fruit, lemon rind, raisins and cinnamon. Cancel the "sauté" function.

3. Cover with lid and set the valve to "seal". Choose "Manual" and adjust to 5 minutes cooking time at high pressure. At the end of the cooking time, use the quick release method to release the pressure.

4. Use a slotted spoon to remove the fruits and place in a bowl.

5. Stir arrowroot into the cooking liquid then transfer the liquid into a high speed blender or food processor. Add cashews to the liquid in the blender. Blend until smooth.

6. Serve the fruits and top with the cashew cream.

Hot Chocolate Fondue (Vegan)

Preparation time: 5 minutes

Cooking time: 2 minutes

Servings: 2-4

Ingredients:

3 1/2 ounces unsweetened coconut milk

3 1/2 ounces dark bittersweet chocolate (at least 70% chocolate)

1 teaspoon Amaretto liquor (optional)

1 teaspoon sugar (optional)

Water

Directions:

1. Add 2 cups of water to the Instant Pot then set the trivet inside.

2. In a small casserole dish that can fit into the Instant Pot, combine the chocolate and coconut milk. Add the optional ingredients, if using. Place casserole dish, uncovered into the Instant Pot.

3. Cover with lid and set the valve to "seal". Choose "Manual" and adjust to 2 minutes cooking time at high pressure. At the end of the cooking time, use the quick release method to release the pressure.

4. Carefully open the lid then use tongs to pull out the casserole dish. Immediately stir the contents vigorously with a fork for about 1 minute.

5. As you keep stirring, the chocolate will become smooth and thick. Do not add any cold ingredients at this point.

6. Serve hot, with sliced fresh fruit or cookies.

Easy Custard (Clean eating)

Preparation time: 20 minutes

Cooking time: 40 minutes

Servings: 6-8

Ingredients:

1 cup fresh cream

1 cup whole milk

Zest from 1 lemon

6 egg yolks

3/4 cup white sugar

Directions:

1. Place a cast iron skillet on medium heat. Add the cream, milk and lemon zest. Cook with occasional stirring until bubbly then turn of the heat. Set aside to cool for about 30 minutes.

2. Meanwhile, add 2 cups of water to the Instant Pot and set aside.

3. Whisk egg yolks and sugar together in a mixing bowl, until sugar dissolves. Slowly pour in the cooled milk/cream mixture and gently incorporate with the whisk.

4. Pour the mixture through a strainer into another bowl.

5. Pour the mixture into ramekins and cover with foil. Arrange as many ramekins as possible in the steamer basket, making sure they are all sitting upright. Carefully lower the basket into the Instant Pot. If possible, stack additional ramekins on the first layer.

6. Cover with lid and set the valve to "seal". Choose "Manual" and adjust to 10 minutes cooking time at high pressure. At the end of the cooking time, allow the pressure to release naturally.

7. Carefully open the lid and remove the ramekins. Custards will still be very soft. Set aside to cool, uncovered for 35-45 minutes. When cooled, cover with plastic wrap and refrigerate.

8. Serve with fresh fruit and drizzle with fruit syrup.

Amaretti Stuffed Peaches (Clean eating)

A sweet, tart and crunchy dessert.

Preparation time: 10 minutes

Cooking time: 10 minutes

Servings: 6

Ingredients:

4 tablespoons sugar

1 cup red wine

2 tablespoons almonds

8 Amaretti Cookies, crumbled

1 teaspoon lemon zest

2 tablespoons olive oil

3 peaches, mature but firm

Directions:

1. Add sugar and water to the Instant Pot. Place the steamer basket inside.

2. Crumble the cookies and combine with almonds. Stir in lemon zest and olive oil.

3. Wash peaches very well, slice in half, remove the pith and create a wide cavity. Fill the cavity of each peach half with the cookie/almond filling. Dust the top with some of the filling. Arrange peach halves in the steamer basket

4. Cover with lid and set the valve to "seal". Choose "Manual" and adjust to 3 minutes cooking time at high pressure. At the end of the cooking time, use the quick release method to release the pressure.

5. Using tongs, remove the peaches and transfer to plates.

6. Press the "sauté" function and cook the red wine in the Instant pot until syrupy. Drizzle the syrup on the peaches.

7. Serve with vanilla ice cream or whipped cream.

Instant Pot Rice Pudding (Clean eating)

If you love rice pudding, this is a dish to try.

Preparation time: 5 minutes

Cooking time: 5 minutes

Servings: 8

Ingredients:

1 cup Arborio rice

1/4 teaspoon salt

1 1/2 cups water

1/2 cup sugar

2 cups whole milk, divided

2 eggs

1/2 teaspoon of vanilla extract

3/4 cup raisins

Directions:

1. In the Instant Pot, combine rice, salt and water.

2. Cover with lid and set the valve to "seal". Choose "Manual" and adjust to 3 minutes cooking time at high pressure. At the end of the cooking time, use the 10-minute Natural Release.

3. Open the lid carefully, add sugar and 1 1/2 cups of milk then stir to combine.

4. In a small bowl, whisk together the eggs, 1/2 cup milk and the vanilla. Pour the mixture through a fine mesh strainer into the Instant Pot.

5. Press the "sauté" function and cook with constant stirring, until the mixture is bubbly. Turn off the Instant Pot and stir in the raisins.

6. Pour into serving dishes and place in the fridge to chill. The pudding will become more solid as it cools.

7. Serve with a topping of whipped cream and sprinkled with cinnamon.

Caribbean Rice Pudding (Clean eating)
Arborio rice is combined with coconut milk and studded with pineapple pieces in this colorful rice pudding.

Preparation time: 5 minutes

Cooking time: 5 minutes

Servings: 8

Ingredients:

1 cup Arborio rice

1 tablespoon coconut oil

1 1/2 cups water

1/4 teaspoon salt

1 (14-ounce) can coconut milk

1/2 cup of sugar

2 eggs

1/2 cup of milk

1/2 teaspoon of vanilla extract

1 can pineapple tidbits, drained, cut in half

Directions:

1. Add rice, coconut oil, water and salt to the Instant pot.

2. Cover with lid and set the valve to "seal". Choose "Soup" and adjust to 3 minutes cooking time at high pressure. At the end of the cooking time, use the 10-minute Natural Release.

3. Open the lid carefully, add sugar and coconut milk then stir to combine.

4. In a small bowl, whisk together the eggs, 1/2 cup milk and the vanilla. Pour the mixture through a fine mesh strainer into the Instant Pot.

5. Press the "sauté" function and cook with constant stirring, until the mixture is bubbly. Turn off the Instant Pot and stir in the pineapple tidbits.

6. Pour into serving dishes and place in the fridge to chill. The pudding will become more solid as it cools.

7. Serve with a topping of whipped cream and toasted coconut.

Classic Pumpkin Pie (Clean eating)
This is an adaptation of the tradition dessert we all love.

Preparation time: 20 minutes

Cooking time: 35 minutes

Servings: 6-8

Ingredients:

1/3 cup toasted pecans, chopped

6 Pecan Sandies cookies, crushed

2 tablespoons butter, melted

1 1/2 teaspoon pumpkin pie spice

1/2 teaspoon salt

1/2 cup light brown sugar

1 egg, beaten

1/2 cup evaporated milk

1 1/2 cups solid pack pumpkin

Directions:

1. Coat a 7-inch springform pan with non-stick spray.

2. In a bowl, mix together chopped toasted pecans, cookie crumbs and butter. Spread the mixture evenly in the bottom of the springform pan and about 1 inch up the sides. Place in your freezer for 10 minutes.

3. In another large bowl, mix together pumpkin pie spice, salt and sugar. Whisk in the egg, followed by milk and pumpkin.

4. Pour the filling into the pie crust in the springform pan. Cover the pan with aluminum foil.

5. Pour 1 cup of water into the Instant Pot then fit the trivet inside. Make a foil sling and use it to lower the springform pan unto the trivet. Fold the foil sling down so you can close the lid of the Instant Pot.

6. Cover with lid and set the valve to "seal". Choose "Manual" and adjust to 35 minutes cooking time at high pressure. At the end of the cooking time, use the 10-minute Natural Release.

7. Carefully remove the lid. Remove the pie and check the middle if it is set. If it is not done, cook for 5 minutes more at high pressure.

8. When done, transfer the springform pan to a wire rack. When the pie is cool, cover it with plastic wrap and refrigerate for least 4 hours.

Spicy Apple Crunch (Clean eating)

You can also make this with peaches instead of apples.

Preparation time: 10 minutes

Cooking time: 17 minutes

Servings: 3

Ingredients:

1 cup dry bread crumbs (whole grain bread)

1/2 teaspoon cinnamon

1/4 cup sugar

1 lemon (juice and zest)

3 apples, sliced

1/4 cup butter, melted

2 cups water

Directions:

1. Coat a 6-inch baking dish with butter.

2. In a bowl, combine bread crumbs, cinnamon, sugar, lemon juice and lemon zest.

3. Place a single layer of apple slices in the baking dish, spread with bread crumbs mixture. Continue layering apple slices and bread crumbs mixture until you run out.

4. Pour melted butter over everything then firmly cover the baking dish with foil.

5. Add 2 cups of water to the Instant Pot then set the trivet inside. Place the baking dish on the trivet.

6. Cover with lid and set the valve to "seal". Choose "Manual" and adjust to 17 minutes cooking time at high pressure. At the end of the cooking time, allow the pressure to release naturally.

7. Carefully remove the lid, take out the baking dish and remove the foil. Transfer to the fridge to cool.

Easy Bread Pudding (Clean eating)

Preparation time: 10 minutes

Cooking time: 22 minutes

Servings: 6

Ingredients:

1 tablespoon butter

4 slices day-old, whole wheat bread, crusts trimmed, cut in cubes

1/2 cup chopped walnuts

1/2 cup golden raisins

Zest of 1/2 orange

1/4 teaspoon salt

1/2 cup packed light brown sugar

1/2 teaspoon cinnamon

2 eggs, lightly beaten

2 cups warm milk

1/2 teaspoon vanilla

3 cups water

Cinnamon

Directions:

1. Coat a (5-6 cup) soufflé dish with butter. Ensure the dish can fit loosely into your Instant Pot.

2. In a small bowl, mix together bread, walnuts, raisins and orange zest. In another bowl, mix together salt, brown sugar, cinnamon, eggs, milk and vanilla.

3. Pour the milk mixture gently into the bread mixture then transfer everything to the prepared soufflé dish. Firmly cover the soufflé dish with foil.

4. Add 3 cups of water to the Instant Pot then set the trivet inside. Place the soufflé dish on the trivet.

5. Cover with lid and set the valve to "seal". Choose "Manual" and adjust to 22 minutes cooking time at high pressure. At the end of the cooking time, use quick release then leave the cooker covered for 20 minutes.

6. Remove the lid, take out the soufflé dish and remove the foil. Transfer to the fridge to cool.

7. Serve with whipped cream and sprinkle with cinnamon

Easy Fruit Jam (Vegan)

Preparation time: 5 minutes

Cooking time: 20 minutes

Servings: 4 cups

Ingredients:

4 cups blackberries, raspberries, strawberries

1 cup water

3 teaspoons pectin

1 cup sugar

1 teaspoon lime or lemon juice

Directions:

1. Combine the fruit and water in the Instant Pot.

2. Cover with lid and set the valve to "seal". Choose "Manual" and adjust to 10 minutes cooking time at Low pressure. At the end of the cooking time, use the quick release method to release the pressure.

3. Open the lid and use a potato masher to mash the fruit.

4. Stir in the pectin, sugar and lime or lemon juice.

5. Press "sauté" and let simmer with occasional stirring, until the jam starts to stick to the spoon, about 8-10 minutes.

6. Spoon the jam into jars. Let cool then cover with airtight lid.

Peachy Butter Spread (Paleo, Gluten free)

This is a sweet spread that goes well with fresh bread or even breakfast oats.

Preparation time: 5 minutes

Cooking time: 6 minutes

Servings: 2 cups

Ingredients:

3 cups diced peaches or nectarines

1 cup water

1 teaspoon of ground cinnamon

1 teaspoon of butter

Directions:

1. In the Instant Pot, combine peaches, water and cinnamon.

2. Cover with lid and set the valve to "seal". Choose "Manual" and adjust to 3 minutes cooking time at high pressure. At the end of the cooking time, use the quick release method to release the pressure.

3. Open the lid and use a potato masher to mash the peaches.

4. Stir in the butter, press "sauté" and let simmer, until reduced to jam-like consistency, about 2-3 minutes.

DIPS AND APPETIZERS

Steamed Artichokes (Paleo, Gluten free)

Preparation time: 5 minutes

Cooking time: 30 minutes

Servings: 2-4

Ingredients:

1 lemon wedge

2 medium-sized whole artichokes

1 cup of water

Directions:

1. Rinse artichokes in water and remove outer leaves that are damaged. Use a sharp knife to trim off the stem and cut off the top third of each artichoke. Immediately rub a lemon wedge on the cut top (this prevents browning).

2. Place a steamer basket or steam rack in your Instant Pot. Add artichokes to the basket then pour in the water.

3. Cover with lid and set the valve to "seal". Choose "Manual" adjust to 20 minutes cooking time at high pressure.

4. At the end of the cooking time, use the 10-minute Natural Release.

5. Using tongs, remove the artichokes then serve with your desired dipping sauce.

Honey Glazed Chicken Wings (Clean eating)

Enjoy the sweetness of honey in this nicely browned and flavorful chicken wings appetizer.

Preparation time: 20 minutes

Cooking time: 25 minutes

Servings: 8

Ingredients:

2 tablespoons sesame oil

2 tablespoons olive oil

12 chicken wings, cut apart at joints

1/2 cup plus 2 tablespoons honey, divided

1/2 cup chicken broth

2 tablespoons sherry

1/4 cup soy sauce

1 teaspoon crushed red pepper flakes

1/4 teaspoon ground ginger

2 garlic cloves, crushed

1/4 cup sesame seeds

Directions:

1. Add oils to the Instant Pot and select the "sauté" function. When hot, add the chicken and brown on all sides. Remove browned chicken and set aside.

2. In the Instant Pot, combine 1/2 cup honey, broth, sherry, soy sauce, red pepper flakes, ginger and garlic. Stir well.

3. Return the chicken to the Instant Pot and mix gently to coat.

4. Cover with lid and set the valve to "seal". Choose "Manual" and adjust to 3 minutes cooking time at high pressure. At the end of the cooking time, use the quick release method to release the pressure.

5. Carefully open the lid and stir the contents. Remove chicken wings and place on a broiler pan.

6. Preheat the broiler. Combine 1/4 of the sauce(in the pot) with the sesame seeds and the remaining honey. Brush this mixture over the chicken.

7. Broil chicken until golden on the first side. Flip over, brush with the mixture again and broil the other side until golden.

Easy Caponata (Clean eating, Gluten free)

A healthy and delicious salad or appetizer.

Preparation time: 15 minutes

Cooking time: 5 minutes

Servings: 8

Ingredients:

1 large eggplant, unpeeled, cut into 1-inch cubes

1 large zucchini squash, unpeeled, sliced thickly

1 onion, diced

2 bell peppers, diced

Extra-virgin olive oil, to taste

3 garlic cloves, minced

Sugar or splenda, to taste

1/4 cup red wine vinegar

1/2 cup finely shredded basil

Directions:

1. In the Instant Pot, add eggplant, zucchini, onion and bell peppers together.

2. Cover with lid and set the valve to "seal". Choose "Manual" and adjust to 5 minutes cooking time at high pressure. At the end of the cooking time, use the quick release method to release the pressure.

3. Transfer the vegetables to a colander to drain excess liquid. Vegetables should be soft and fully cooked.

4. Place vegetables in a bowl, and toss with extra virgin olive oil, garlic, sugar or splenda, red wine vinegar and basil. Mix well and place in refrigerator.

Southern Chicken Dip (Clean eating)

Preparation time: 20 minutes

Cooking time: 18 minutes

Servings: 24

Ingredients:

2 tablespoons olive oil

3 slices bacon, diced

3 garlic cloves, peeled, minced

1 medium white onion, peeled, diced

1/2 cup fresh cilantro, minced

1 pound chicken breast tenders, diced finely

1 teaspoon chili powder

1/2 cup chicken broth

1/4 cup ketchup

1/2 cup salsa

1/2 cup light sour cream

1 cup low-sodium Parmesan cheese, grated

Salt, to taste

Freshly ground black pepper, to taste

Directions:

1. Combine oil and bacon in the Instant Pot then press "sauté". When hot, add garlic, onion and cilantro. Cook until onion is tender, about 3 minutes.

2. Stir in diced chicken, chili powder, chicken broth, ketchup and salsa.

3. Cover with lid and set the valve to "seal". Choose "Manual" and adjust to 6 minutes cooking time at Low pressure. At the end of the cooking time, use the quick release method to release the pressure.

4. Open the lid carefully, press "sauté" and let simmer to thicken the sauce. If you are in a hurry, whisk a little all-purpose flour into the dip and heat through.

5. Add cheese and stir constantly, until melted. Stir in the sour cream then taste for seasoning. If necessary, add salt and pepper.

6. Serve warm with tortilla chips or baked corn.

BBQ Chicken Wings (Clean eating)

Juicy, tender and really great for parties.

Preparation time: 5 minutes

Cooking time: 25 minutes

Servings: 8

Ingredients:

12 chicken wings, cut apart at joints

2 tablespoons cooking oil

1 large onion, chopped

1/4 cup red wine, optional

1 (18-ounce) bottle of barbecue sauce

Directions:

1. Press "sauté", add oil to the Instant Pot and sauté onions till tender.

2. Add chicken wings then cook and stir until browned.

3. Stir in wine and barbecue sauce and ensure chicken is coated.

4. Cover with lid and set the valve to "seal". Choose "Manual" and adjust to 10 minutes cooking time at high pressure. At the end of the cooking time, use the quick release method to release the pressure.

5. Remove the chicken wings to a platter.

6. Press "sauté" and let the sauce simmer until thickened.

7. Serve chicken wings with sauce.

Black Bean Dip (Clean eating, Gluten Free)

Preparation time: 15 minutes

Cooking time: 22 minutes

Servings: 12

Ingredients:

1 cup dried black beans, soaked overnight

4 slices bacon, diced finely

1 tablespoon olive oil

1 small onion, peeled, diced

3 garlic cloves, peeled, minced

2 (4-ounce cans) mild green chilies, chopped finely

1 (14.5-ounce) can diced tomatoes

1/2 teaspoon dried oregano

1 teaspoon chili powder

1/4 cup fresh cilantro, chopped finely

Salt, to taste

1 cup grated low-sodium Parmesan cheese

Directions:

1. Press "sauté" then add bacon and oil to the Instant Pot. Fry until bacon is almost done.

2. Add the onion and cook until soft, about 3 minutes. Add garlic and cook for 30 seconds.

3. Drain the beans and add to the Instant Pot. Add green chilies, tomatoes, oregano and chili powder. Stir well and scrape up any browned bits on the bottom of the pot.

4. Cover with lid and set the valve to "seal". Choose "Manual" and adjust to 12 minutes cooking time at high pressure. At the end of the cooking time, use the 10-minute Natural Release.

5. Open the lid and transfer the contents to a blender or food processor. Add the cilantro then blend until smooth. Taste and add additional salt if necessary.

6. Transfer the dip to a serving bowl and stir in the cheese. Serve warm with baked tortilla chips or corn chips.

Asian Split Pea Soup (Vegan)

A colorful, tasty and soothing appetizer.

Preparation time: 30 minutes

Cooking time: 15 minutes

Servings: 4-5

Ingredients:

2 whole star anise "flowers"

10 small dried shiitake mushrooms (about 3/4 ounce)

2 cups boiling water

1 tablespoon peanut oil

1 onion, finely diced

2 teaspoons minced garlic

5 scallions, thinly sliced, white and green parts separated

1/4 cup dry sherry

1 1/2 cups split peas, sorted, rinsed

4 cups of water

2 inches piece of ginger, finely chopped

1/2 teaspoon salt

2-3 tablespoons Japanese soy sauce

1 bunch loosely packed watercress leaves, chopped coarsely

2-3 teaspoons Asian (toasted) sesame oil

Directions:

1. Combine star anise and shiitake in a large bowl. Pour the 2 cups of boiling water on top. Cover and set aside until the shiitake are soft enough to cut, about 10 minutes. Use a slotted spoon to remove star anise and mushrooms. Slice the caps thinly and discard the stems. Set the star anise, mushrooms and the soaking water aside.

2. Press "sauté" and heat oil in the Instant Pot. Add the onion, garlic and white part of scallions. Cook with frequent stirring, until softened about 2 minutes.

3. Stir in sherry and cook with constant stirring, for about 30 seconds, or until sherry evaporates.

4. Add the split peas, 4 cups of water, star anise, sliced shiitake, ginger and salt. Pour in the reserved soaking liquid, (leaving behind any grit in the bowl).

5. Cover with lid and set the valve to "seal". Choose "Manual" and adjust to 10 minutes cooking time at high pressure. At the end of the cooking time, allow the pressure to release naturally.

6. Open the lid carefully and stir in soy sauce, watercress, scallion greens and toasted sesame oil to taste.

Tropical Relish (Clean eating)

Preparation time: 10 minutes

Cooking time: 12 minutes

Servings: 12

Ingredients:

1 1/2 cups red or white kidney beans, soaked overnight

4 cups water

2 teaspoons vegetable oil

3/8 cup crushed pineapple, drained

2 tablespoons tahini paste

4 garlic cloves, peeled, minced

1/4 teaspoon ground ginger

1/4 teaspoon dried cumin

1/2 cup fresh cilantro, minced

1/4 teaspoon freshly ground white pepper

Salt, to taste

Directions:

1. Drain beans and add to the Instant Pot with 4 cups of water and the oil.

2. Cover with lid and set the valve to "seal". Choose "Manual" and adjust to 12 minutes cooking time at high pressure. At the end of the cooking time, use the 10-minute Natural Release.

3. Open the lid and drain the beans.

4. Combine the cooked beans with the rest of the ingredients in a food processor or blender. Pulse until mixed but still has chunks.

5. Transfer to a container, cover and refrigerate.

6. Serve as dip for corn chips.

Taco Chips Dip (Clean eating)

Preparation time: 15 minutes

Cooking time: 20 minutes

Servings: 16

Ingredients:

1 cup dried kidney beans, soaked overnight

1/4 cup olive oil

1 large onion, peeled, diced

1 pound of ground beef

2 garlic cloves, peeled, minced

1 cup beef broth

1 (8-ounce) can tomato sauce

1 tablespoon light brown sugar

1 teaspoon crushed red pepper flakes

1 teaspoon ground cumin

2 teaspoons chili powder

Salt, to taste

Directions:

1. Drain beans and set aside.

2. Press "sauté" and heat oil in the Instant Pot. Add onion and sauté until tender, about 3 minutes.

3. Add the ground beef. Stir to break apart and cook until no longer pink. Stir in the garlic.

4. Add beans, broth, tomato sauce, brown sugar, red pepper flakes, cumin and chili powder. Stir well.

5. Cover with lid and set the valve to "seal". Choose "Manual" and adjust to 10 minutes cooking time at high pressure. At the end of the cooking time, use the 10-minute Natural Release.

6. Stir the dip and crush the beans against the walls of the pot. If you want a smooth dip, transfer to a blender or food processor and puree. Taste and add salt if necessary. Serve warm.

END

Thank you for reading my book. If you enjoyed it, won't you please take a moment to leave a good review at your retailer?

Thanks!

Paula Corey